MRCP 1 POCKET BOOK 3

Endocrinology, Gastroenterology, and Nephrology

Colin M Dayan MA MRCP PhD
Christopher S J Probert MD MRCP ILTM
Andrew D Higham MRCP
Helen Paynter MRCP
Philip A Kalra MA MB Chir FRCP MD

First edition 2002

ISBN: 1 901198 855

A catalogue record for this book is available from the British Library.

The information contained within this book was obtained by the author from reliable sources. However, while every effort has been made to ensure its accuracy, no responsibilty for loss, damage or injury occasioned to any person acting or refraining from action as a result of information contained herein can be accepted by the publishers or author.

Typeset by Breeze Limited, Manchester
Printed by MPG Books Limited, Bodmin, Cornwall

CONTENTS

Introduction   vi

Endocrinology
  'Best of Five' Questions   3
  Multiple Choice Questions   13

Gastroenterology
  'Best of Five' Questions   23
  Multiple Choice Questions   33

Nephrology
  'Best of Five' Questions   41
  Multiple Choice Questions   51

Answers and teaching explanations
  Endocrinology   59
  Gastroenterology   77
  Nephrology   87

Revision Checklists
  Endocrinology   103
  Gastroenterology   105
  Nephrology   107

Revision Index   109

INTRODUCTION

PasTest's MRCP Part 1 Pocket Books are designed to help the busy examination candidate to make the most of every opportunity to revise. With this little book in your pocket, it is the work of a moment to open it, choose a question, decide upon your answers and then check the answer. Revising 'on the run' in this manner is both reassuring (if your answer is correct) and stimulating (if you find any gaps in your knowledge).

For quite some time the Royal College of Physicians has been conducting an extensive review of the MRCP Part 1 examination and has recently announced changes to be introduced in May 2002. From an educational point of view both these changes are to be welcomed.

Negative marking (penalty scoring) will be discontinued

From the candidates' point of view, this is an important change because incorrect answers will no longer be penalised by the deduction of marks – they will simply not gain any marks. (From the Examiners' point of view it should improve the reliability of the examination by removing an uncontrollable variable – individual candidates' willingness to venture an answer when they are less than 100% confident.)

A second paper will be introduced in addition to the current 2½ hour, 60 question multiple true/false examination. This will also last for 2½ hours, but consist of 100 questions using a new type of Multiple Choice Question (MCQ) – the one-best answer/'Best of Five' format.

This means that the examination from May 2002 onwards will last all day. Candidates will also need to become familiar with one-best MCQs and the strategies for answering them. However, one-best is a much better design than multiple true/false. They are typically more valid and reliable, so their introduction should be to the advantage of good candidates.

One-best answer/'Best of Five' MCQs
An important characteristic of one-best answer MCQs is that they can be designed to test application of knowledge and clinical problem-solving rather than just the recall of facts.
This should change (for the better) the ways in which candidates prepare for MRCP Part 1.

Each one-best MCQ has a question stem, which usually contains clinical information, followed by five branches. All five branches are typically homologous (e.g. all diagnoses, all laboratory investigations, all antibiotics etc) and should be set out in a logical order (e.g. alphabetical). Candidates are asked to select the ONE branch that is the best answer to the question. A response is not required to the other four branches. The answer sheet is, therefore, slightly different to that used for true/false MCQs.

A good strategy that can be used with many well-written one-best MCQs is to try to reach the correct answer without first scrutinising the five options. If you can then find the answer you have reached in the option list, then you are probably correct.

One-best answer MCQs are quicker to answer than multiple true/false MCQs because only one response is needed for each question. Even though the question stem for one-best answer MCQs is usually longer than for true/false questions, and therefore takes a little longer to read carefully, it is reasonable to set more one-best than true/false MCQs for the same exam duration – in this instance 60 true/false and 100 one-best are used in exams of 2 hours.

Application of Knowledge and Clinical Problem-Solving

Unlike true/false MCQs, which test mainly the recall of knowledge, one-best answer questions test application and problem-solving. This makes them more effective test items and is one of the reasons why testing time can be reduced. In order to answer these questions correctly, it is necessary to apply basic knowledge – not just be able to remember it. Furthermore, candidates who cannot reach the correct answer by applying their knowledge are much less likely to be able to choose the right answer by guessing than they were with true/false MCQs. This gives a big advantage to the best candidates, who have good knowledge and can apply it in clinical situations.

Multiple Choice Questions

Each question consists of an initial statement followed by five possible completions, ABCDE. There is no restriction on the number of true or false items in a question. It is possible for all items in a question to be true or for all to be false. The most important points of technique are:

1. Read the question carefully and be sure you understand it.
2. Mark your response clearly, correctly and accurately.
3. The best possible way to obtain a good mark is to have as wide a knowledge as possible of the topics being tested in the examination.

To get the best value from the MCQ sections you should commit yourself to an answer for each item before you check the correct answer. It is only by being sure of your own responses that you can ascertain which questions you would find difficult in the examination.

Books like the ones in this series, which consist of 'Best of Five' and MCQs in subject categories, can help you to focus on specific topics and to isolate your weaknesses. You should plan a revision timetable to help you spread your time evenly over the range of subjects likely to appear in the examination. PasTest's Essential Revision Notes for MRCP by P Kalra will provide you with essential notes on all aspects of the syllabus.

ENDOCRINOLOGY

'Best of Five' and MCQs

Dr C M Dayan MA MRCP PhD
Consultant Senior Lecturer
University Division of Medicine
Bristol Royal Infirmary
Bristol

ENDOCRINOLOGY: 'BEST OF FIVE' QUESTIONS

For each of the questions select the ONE most appropriate answer from the option provided.

1.1 A 29-year-old primigravida woman with hyperemesis at 9 weeks of pregnancy has her thyroid function tests measured because of a resting tachycardia. These show a TSH = < 0.1 mU/l, free T3 = 6.8 pmol/l (normal range 2.5–5.2). There is no previous history of thyroid disease. On examination she has minimal non-tender thyroid enlargement. Ultrasound reveals a single live conceptus. Which one of the following is the most appropriate management strategy?

- [ ] A Advise termination of pregnancy
- [ ] B Commence treatment immediately with propylthiouracil with a view to dose adjustments through the remainder of pregnancy
- [ ] C Commence treatment immediately with propylthiouracil with a view to performing subtotal thyroidectomy in the second trimester of pregnancy
- [x] D Withhold any antithyroid treatment and repeat thyroid function testing in 3 weeks
- [ ] E Withhold any antithyroid treatment pending a radionucleotide thyroid scan to exclude transient thyroiditis

1.2 A 54-year-old man who has had transphenoidal surgery and external beam radiotherapy for a nonfunctioning pituitary tumour 6 years previously has been seen by his GP recently, feeling increasingly tired with loss of libido. Tests done at that consultation showed testosterone = < 0.1 nmol/l (normal range 10–30), TSH = 2.3 mU/l (normal range 0.4–4.5). He now presents to casualty with vomiting. BP 90/60 mmHg Na⁺ 121 mmol/l K⁺ 3.8 mmol/l. He is on no medication. Which one of the following is the most appropriate immediate course of action?

- [ ] A Admit the patient for an insulin stress test to assess pituitary function
- [ ] B Immediate treatment with intramuscular testosterone
- [ ] C Immediate treatment with thyroxine
- [ ] D Rehydrate with saline and then arrange a short synacthen test
- [x] E Short synacthen testing followed by immediate treatment with hydrocortisone

1.3 **In treatment of an acute asthmatic attack, beta agonists, and corticosteroids are frequently used. Which one of the following is true of the molecular mechanism by which these agents act?**

☐ A Beta agonists have a prolonged action because they act by both modulating gene transcription and an intracellular second messenger

☐ B Both agents act quickly because they act via an intracellular second messenger

☐ C Both agents act quickly because they have specific cellular receptors

☐ D Corticosteroids act more slowly because they act via modulating gene transcription

☐ E Corticosteroids have a prolonged action because they are lipid soluble

1.4 **In a hypertensive individual, which one of the following is the likely finding in a patient with renal artery stenosis and is helpful in distinguishing the condition from Conn's syndrome?**

☐ A A high aldosterone level

☐ B A high renin and a high aldosterone level

☐ C A high renin level

☐ D A low aldosterone level

☐ E A low renin and a high aldosterone level

1.5 **An overweight 43-year-old woman is referred with the clinical appearance of Cushing's syndrome and a blood pressure of 170/90 mmHg. The best initial test to distinguish this diagnosis from simple obesity would be?**

☐ A An ACTH level

☐ B An adrenal MRI scan

☐ C A midnight salivary cortisol level

☐ D Serum potassium and bicarbonate

☐ E 24-hour urinary free cortisol

1.6 A 60-year-old gentleman with type 2 diabetes has a myocardial infarction. He is treated initially with an intravenous infusion of insulin. He has an episode of left ventricular failure and is started on an ACE inhibitor. He has a degree of renal dysfunction with a creatinine of 147 μmol/l which is stable. He is usually on 80 mg bd of gliclazide. You notice that his HbA_{1c} is 11.2% and on dietician review there is not much that can be changed. Which one of the following is the most appropriate therapy for his diabetes?

- ☐ A Acarbose
- ☐ B Basal bolus insulin
- ☐ C Increase gliclazide to 160 mg bd
- ☐ D Metformin
- ☐ E Rosiglitazone

1.7 A 32-year-old man who has had Type 1 diabetes for 12 years reports episodes of confusion occurring without warning. On one of these occasions, the blood sugar level on home testing was 2.5 mmol/l. The single best advice to help this patient for the future would be?

- ☐ A To eat every 2 hours
- ☐ B To eat less carbohydrate with each meal
- ☐ C To increase his insulin at night and reduce it during the day for 3 months
- ☐ D To reduce his insulin to maintain relatively high blood sugars (8–15 mmol/l) for at least 3 months
- ☐ E To test his blood sugar a minimum of four times daily every day

1.8 In a patient with diabetes and microalbuminuria, the most important element of management to preserve renal function is?

- ☐ A Aggressive management of hyperlipidaemia
- ☐ B Aggressive management of hypertension
- ☐ C A low protein diet
- ☐ D Avoidance of diuretic use
- ☐ E To improve glycaemic control

1.9 In a 52-year-old man with acromegaly and moderate sized (1.5 cm) pituitary tumour, the most appropriate first line of therapy would be?

- ☐ A Bromocriptine therapy
- ☐ B External beam radiotherapy
- ☐ C Octreotide therapy
- ☐ D Trans-sphenoidal surgery
- ☐ E Yttrium implants into the pituitary

1.10 Appropriate hormone replacement medication for a 28-year-old woman with primary adrenocortical failure (Addison's disease) would be?

- ☐ A Dexamethasone 0.5 mg daily alone
- ☐ B Hydrocortisone 10 mg mane and fludrocortisone 100 μg mane
- ☐ C Hydrocortisone 10 mg mane, 5 mg pm and fludrocortisone 100 μg mane
- ☐ D Hydrocortisone 50 mg bd and fludrocortisone 100 μg mane
- ☐ E Prednisolone 15 mg mane and fludrocortisone 100 μg mane

1.11 In an individual known to have the genetic mutation responsible for multiple endocrine neoplasia type 2, which one of the following describes the two most important elements in management?

- ☐ A Prophylactic thyroidectomy and bilateral adrenalectomy
- ☐ B Prophylactic thyroidectomy and regular pituitary imaging
- ☐ C Prophylactic thyroidectomy and regular screening for phaeochromocytoma
- ☐ D Regular thyroid imaging and regular screening for phaeochromocytoma
- ☐ E Regular thyroid and pituitary imaging

1.12 **A 23-year-old woman presents concerned about increased hair growth. She is noted to have dark facial and lower abdominal hairs. She menstruates regularly but her cycle length varies from 3–6 weeks. Which one of the following is correct?**

- ☐ A   A benign course is very likely in such cases
- ☐ B   Clitoromegaly is frequently observed in such cases
- ☐ C   If the diagnosis were polycystic ovary syndrome, recent onset of hair growth would be expected
- ☐ D   Radiological imaging for a tumour of the ovary should routinely be performed in all such cases
- ☐ E   Testosterone levels would be expected in the low normal male range in such cases

1.13 **A 39-year-old man presents with a two-week history of polydipsia and polyuria. He is found to have a random glucose of 17.3 mmol/l. There are no ketones in the urine. He denies recent weight loss or vomiting. His BMI is 24.7 kg/m^2. Which one of the following is correct?**

- ☐ A   As in B. but review in three months is more appropriate to assess progress
- ☐ B   He could be started on a sulphonylurea, taught to test his own capillary glucose levels and be reassessed in one month
- ☐ C   He should be admitted to hospital urgently to commence insulin therapy
- ☐ D   He should be referred to a dietitian and reviewed after three months of diet and exercise therapy
- ☐ E   The optimal therapy is metformin

1.14 **Which one of the following is true regarding carbohydrate metabolism after 48 hours of fasting?**

- ☐ A   Amino acids are an increasingly important source of substrates for glucose synthesis
- ☐ B   Fatty acids provide 15–20% of the substrates for glucose synthesis
- ☐ C   Glucagon levels are rising
- ☐ D   Ketonuria is rare
- ☐ E   Liver glycogen is an important source of glucose

1.15 **A 23-year-old man is found on routine screening to have a cholesterol level of 11.3 mmol/l, a triglyceride level of 1.2 mmol/l and a HDL of 1.1 mmol/l. His mother died aged 45 of a heart attack. Which one of the following is most appropriate in this case?**

☐ A Excess alcohol is a possible cause

☐ B He should have a three month trial of dietary advice before commencing lipid lowering therapy

☐ C Treatment should be begun with a 'fibrate'

☐ D Treatment should be begun with a 'statin'

☐ E Undiagnosed diabetes mellitus is a likely cause

1.16 **A 64-year-old lady is noted to have a corrected calcium level of 2.85 mmol/l during blood testing for 'tiredness'. Which one of the following statements is most appropriate in this case?**

☐ A A parathyroid hormone level in the high normal range makes hyperparathyroidism unlikely

☐ B A raised alkaline phosphatase level suggests bony metastases

☐ C Hyperparathyroidism and malignancy account for 90% of cases

☐ D If it is due to hyperparathyroidism, parathyroidectomy is invariably required

☐ E If the patient is asymptomatic, no further investigation is required

1.17 **Growth hormone (GH) therapy in adults. Which one of the following statements is correct?**

☐ A Can improve patients' mood

☐ B Currently is associated with a small but appreciable risk of Creutzfeldt–Jacob disease

☐ C Is associated with weight loss

☐ D Is contraindicated in patients with pituitary tumours

☐ E Should be monitored with GH day curves

1.18 A 78-year-old lady is seen in A&E with right-sided loin pain radiating to her groin and the A&E staff report a capillary blood glucose of 9 mmol/l. On further questioning a history of polyuria and polydipsia is elicited, which one diagnosis below would unify these clinical and laboratory findings?

☐ A Autoimmune polyglandular syndrome type 2 (Schmidt's syndrome)

☐ B Primary hyperparathyroidism

☐ C Pyelonephritis

☐ D Somatostatinoma

☐ E Type 2 diabetes

1.19 In the diabetic clinic you see a 47-year-old woman of Caribbean extraction, she has not been well for the last six months. She reports being extremely tired. She has lost 2 kg in weight. She has thrush and has suffered from recurrent urinary tract infections. Home monitoring tests (using a capillary blood glucose monitor) are mainly in double figures but the pre-clinic HbA_{1c} is 7.3%. Which one of the following tests would best help clarify the inconsistency between the clinical picture and the HbA_{1c} value?

☐ A Fasting blood glucose

☐ B HIV test

☐ C Renal ultrasound

☐ D Repeat HbA_{1c} test

☐ E Sickle cell screen

1.20 You see a 42-year-lady who has had type 1 diabetes since the age of 15. On her last visit to the diabetic clinic she was commenced on therapy for microalbuminuria but despite perseverance is plagued by a dry cough, which one of the following is the likely culprit?

☐ A Atenolol

☐ B Captopril

☐ C Doxazosin

☐ D Losartan

☐ E Nifedipine

1.21 **A 20-year-old lady is referred to the endocrine clinic with a six month history of sweating and diarrhoea. She is otherwise well. Her father and grandmother died in middle age but she is unsure of the reason why. On examination, no abnormality could be found. Which one of the following diagnoses would it be important to exclude?**

☐ A   Cushing's disease

☐ B   Graves' disease

☐ C   Growth hormone secreting pituitary tumour

☐ D   Medullary thyroid carcinoma

☐ E   Premature menopause

1.22 **A 24-year-old female presents to her GP complaining of a sore throat, fevers, myalgia and a painful neck. She says she is very shaky and sweating more than usual. She has been getting some palpitations. TFT show TSH 0.1, free T4 28, free T3 7.2. She is referred to the endocrine clinic. By the time she has her appointment she is much better. She has repeat blood tests which get lost but a TSH is done which is 9.6. Select the most likely diagnosis from the list below.**

☐ A   Drug induced hypothyroidism

☐ B   Graves' disease

☐ C   Post partum thyroiditis

☐ D   Subacute thyroiditis

☐ E   Toxic multinodular goitre

1.23 **An obese (BMI=34) 42-year-old man who works in a dress shop is referred to the diabetic clinic following failure to control his blood sugars on diet alone. He has been working hard at the lifestyle changes of diet and exercise. He has managed to lose 4 kg in weight over the last six months. The time has come when he needs further therapy to try to achieve good glycaemic control, which one of these would be the most appropriate to start with?**

☐ A   Acarbose

☐ B   Gliclazide

☐ C   Metformin

☐ D   Phenformin

☐ E   Rosiglitazone

1.24   A 28-year-old woman presents with secondary amenorrhoea for 12 months. LH, FSH, testosterone and prolactin levels are measured and a *Provera* test is performed. Which one of the following combination of results would be most consistent with a diagnosis of polycystic ovarian syndrome?

☐   A   A high FSH (> 20 iu/l) and a mildly raised prolactin

☐   B   A high FSH (> 20 iu/l) and an undetectable testosterone level

☐   C   A moderately raised LH and no withdrawal bleed following *Provera* challenge

☐   D   A moderately raised LH level and a positive withdrawal bleed following *Provera* challenge

☐   E   Undetectable LH and FSH levels and a raised prolactin

1.25   A 30-year-old female with maturity onset diabetes of the young presents to the diabetic clinic because she is 12 weeks pregnant. Her glycaemic control is excellent with an HbA_{1c} of 5.7% on gliclazide 80 mg twice a day. How would you manage her?

☐   A   Change gliclazide to glibenclamide

☐   B   Continue present management

☐   C   Increase gliclazide to 160 mg bd

☐   D   Replace gliclazide with basal bolus insulin

☐   E   Replace gliclazide with Mixtard insulin bd

ENDOCRINOLOGY: MULTIPLE CHOICE QUESTIONS

Mark your answers with a tick (True) or a cross (False) in the box provided.

1.26 Craniopharyngioma

- ☐ A rarely presents in adulthood
- ☐ B may cause diabetes insipidus without anterior pituitary failure
- ☐ C may cause optic atrophy
- ☐ D rarely recurs after surgery in adults
- ☐ E is associated with suprasellar calcification

1.27 The following are true of insulin-like growth factor-1 (IGF-1):

- ☐ A the site of IGF-1 synthesis is unknown
- ☐ B serum levels are low in acromegaly
- ☐ C serum levels are low in starvation
- ☐ D its serum concentration is ten-fold lower than insulin
- ☐ E there is a single specific IGF binding protein in serum

1.28 Growth hormone (GH) secretion is stimulated by

- ☐ A somatostatin
- ☐ B glucose
- ☐ C amino acids
- ☐ D hexapeptides related to metenkephalins
- ☐ E sleep

1.29 In hypopituitarism

- ☐ A selective gonadotrophin deficiency may be present
- ☐ B concomitant diabetes insipidus (DI) may be masked by anterior pituitary failure
- ☐ C adrenal steroid replacement must be started before thyroid replacement
- ☐ D mineralocorticoid replacement is usually necessary
- ☐ E in men, androgen replacement will cause masculinisation and restore fertility

1.30 Acromegaly

- [ ] A   is rarely caused by a pituitary tumour larger than 1 cm
- [ ] B   is best diagnosed by a fasting GH level
- [ ] C   is not associated with elevations in other pituitary hormones
- [ ] D   may be associated with kidney stones
- [ ] E   is associated with colonic polyps

1.31 Antidiuretic hormone (ADH)

- [ ] A   is synthesised in the posterior pituitary
- [ ] B   is a cyclic octapeptide
- [ ] C   circulates in the blood stream bound to neurophysin
- [ ] D   is released by carbamazepine
- [ ] E   is released by ethanol

1.32 The following are true of diabetes insipidus (DI):

- [ ] A   serum sodium is typically above 140 mmol/l
- [ ] B   it may be caused by lithium
- [ ] C   the congenital nephrogenic form shows autosomal dominant inheritance
- [ ] D   the nephrogenic form may be aggravated by thiazide diuretics
- [ ] E   in the central form (cranial DI), vasopressin replacement is essential for survival

1.33 Galactorrhoea

- [ ] A   is often caused by antidepressants
- [ ] B   may be caused by anti-emetics
- [ ] C   should prompt a search for occult malignancy
- [ ] D   is associated with chronic liver disease
- [ ] E   is most commonly due to a pituitary microadenoma in women

1.34   In anorexia nervosa

☐ A   loss of pubic hair occurs

☐ B   patients may present with primary amenorrhoea

☐ C   luteinizing hormone (LH) levels are elevated

☐ D   the erythrocyte sedimentation rate (ESR) is high

☐ E   cortisol levels are low

1.35   The following statements are true:

☐ A   levels of sex-hormone binding globulin are increased in Klinefelter's syndrome

☐ B   hypogonadotrophic hypogonadism may be associated with anosmia

☐ C   there is a high risk of seminoma in the testicular feminisation syndrome

☐ D   azoospermia is invariable in Klinefelter's syndrome

☐ E   Klinefelter's syndrome causes hypogonadotrophic hypogonadism

1.36   In Graves' disease

☐ A   the eye signs usually improve when hyperthyroidism is controlled by antithyroid drugs

☐ B   levels of thyroid-stimulating hormone (TSH) are normal

☐ C   neonatal hyperthyroidism may result from transplacental passage of maternal thyroxine

☐ D   the thyroid is stimulated by antimicrosomal antibodies

☐ E   amenorrhoea may occur

1.37   Features of primary autoimmune hypothyroidism include

☐ A   increased incidence of type 1 diabetes and Addison's disease

☐ B   pretibial myxoedema

☐ C   multiple serous effusions

☐ D   ataxia

☐ E   paranoia and delusions

1.38   Thyrotoxicosis

- ☐ A   with a markedly raised ESR suggests subacute (de Quervain's) thyroiditis
- ☐ B   without a raised thyroidal radioiodine uptake may occur after pregnancy
- ☐ C   is best treated with surgery
- ☐ D   may cause diarrhoea
- ☐ E   may cause intermittent muscle paralysis

1.39   The following statements are true:

- ☐ A   total thyroxine levels rise in normal pregnancy
- ☐ B   TSH levels are low in hyperemesis gravidarum
- ☐ C   amiodarone may cause hyper- or hypothyroidism
- ☐ D   hypothyroidism may develop during treatment with interferon alpha
- ☐ E   free T3 and T4 levels fall in acute illness but TSH rises

1.40   The following are true of G-proteins:

- ☐ A   they are involved in intracellular signalling via cyclic AMP
- ☐ B   they hydrolyse ATP when activated
- ☐ C   activating mutations may cause growth hormone secreting pituitary tumours
- ☐ D   activating mutations are seen in multiple endocrine neoplasia syndrome Type II
- ☐ E   inactivating mutations may cause pseudohypoparathyroidism

1.41   Common features of Cushing's syndrome due to adrenal carcinoma include

- ☐ A   retarded growth in children
- ☐ B   clitoromegaly
- ☐ C   subconjunctival oedema
- ☐ D   marked hyperpigmentation
- ☐ E   supraclavicular fat pads

1.42   Atrial natriuretic peptide (ANP)

- ☐ A   is synthesised in the juxtaglomerular apparatus of the kidney
- ☐ B   is released in response to hypervolaemia
- ☐ C   promotes sodium retention in the renal tubule
- ☐ D   is itself a vasoconstrictor
- ☐ E   induces salt craving

1.43   The following features suggest inadequate glucocorticoid replacement in Addison's disease:

- ☐ A   insomnia
- ☐ B   tiredness
- ☐ C   loss of appetite
- ☐ D   hypokalaemia
- ☐ E   total daily hydrocortisone dosage of 10 mg

1.44   In congenital adrenal hyperplasia (CAH)

- ☐ A   21-hydroxylase deficiency is the commonest variety
- ☐ B   virilisation may be prevented by glucocorticoid treatment
- ☐ C   adrenal crisis may occur within a few days of birth
- ☐ D   blood 17-hydroxyprogesterone concentrations are greatly increased
- ☐ E   severe hypoglycaemia may occur

1.45   Idiopathic hypoparathyroidism is associated with

- ☐ A   increased incidence of Addison's disease
- ☐ B   chronic mucocutaneous candidiasis
- ☐ C   basal ganglia calcification, commonly causing Parkinsonism
- ☐ D   short fourth and fifth metacarpals
- ☐ E   good response of hypocalcaemia to calcium and vitamin D treatment

1.46 **The following statements are true of Paget's disease:**

- ☐ A hydroxycholecalciferol is a useful treatment
- ☐ B it is believed to be primarily a disease of osteoblasts
- ☐ C deafness may occur
- ☐ D serum alkaline phosphatase levels reflect disease activity
- ☐ E extensive disease on bone scan is an indication for treatment

1.47 **Features of the multiple endocrine neoplasia (MEN) syndrome type 1 include**

- ☐ A parathyroid hyperplasia
- ☐ B multiple neuromata around the eyes and mouth
- ☐ C acromegaly
- ☐ D medullary carcinoma of the thyroid
- ☐ E profuse watery diarrhoea

1.48 **In the differential diagnosis of hypoglycaemia**

- ☐ A high C-peptide concentrations in the presence of hypoglycaemia suggest factitious insulin administration
- ☐ B a high ratio of proinsulin to insulin in a fasting blood sample is a feature of insulinoma
- ☐ C nesidioblastosis should be considered in the neonate or infant
- ☐ D the tolbutamide test is useful in the diagnosis of insulinoma
- ☐ E a 72-hour fast fails to produce hypoglycaemia in up to 20% of insulinomas

1.49 **Phaeochromocytoma**

- ☐ A is excluded by a normal CT scan of the adrenals
- ☐ B may secrete dopamine
- ☐ C is associated with islet-cell tumours
- ☐ D pending surgery, should be treated by β-blockade
- ☐ E may be localised on an IVP

1.50   The following statements are true:

- ☐ A   calcitonin-gene related peptide has a potent calcium-lowering effect
- ☐ B   diarrhoea is common in the gastrinoma syndrome
- ☐ C   DDAVP is a powerful vasoconstrictor
- ☐ D   thromboembolic disease is common in the glucagonoma syndrome
- ☐ E   high gastrin levels are associated with pernicious anaemia

GASTROENTEROLOGY

'Best of Five'

Christopher S J Probert, MD MRCP ILTM
Consultant Senior Lecturer
University Division of Medicine
Bristol Royal Infirmary
Bristol

MCQs

Andrew D Higham MRCP
Training Fellow and Honorary Senior Registrar
Department of Gastroenterology
Hope Hospital
Salford

2.6   **A 26-year-old woman presents with a six-month history of colicky lower abdominal pain associated with loose stool. The stool is accompanied by mucus but not blood. Despite urgency she has noted incomplete evacuation and the need to strain during defaecation. Her weight is increasing. During the last 12 months, she has moved house and then lost her job through redundancy. Bearing in mind the MOST likely diagnosis, what would you do next ?**

☐ A   Arrange a barium enema

☐ B   Arrange a colonoscopy

☐ C   Reassure her with explanation of the diagnosis, without further investigation

☐ D   Refer to a dietitian

☐ E   Refer to a debt counsellor

2.7   **A 76-year-old man has a PEG in place after a stroke. He presents with vomiting (possibly complicated by aspiration) and apparent abdominal pain after being fed by the PEG. Which one of the following is the explanation?**

☐ A   Brain tumour

☐ B   Drug toxicity

☐ C   Hiatus hernia

☐ D   Migration of the PEG with pyloric obstruction

☐ E   Overfeeding

2.8   **A 25-year-old man presents with a history of severe reflux oesophagitis. Which one of the following is the treatment of choice?**

☐ A   Antacids only

☐ B   Antireflux surgery

☐ C H_2 receptor antagonist

☐ D   High dose PPI, reducing later

☐ E   Prokinetic therapy

2.9 After being treated for bleeding oesophageal varices, you discover an alcoholic patient with ascites has deteriorating renal function. His creatinine is rising each day and his urine output is falling. How would you treat him?

- ☐ A   CAPD
- ☐ B   Dopamine infusion
- ☐ C   Intravenous saline
- ☐ D   Paracentesis/albumin/glypressin
- ☐ E   Spironolactone

2.10 A 26-year-old woman presents to A&E with vomiting and drowsiness. She had been unwell for several days. On examination, she has deep jaundice, blood around the lips, sluggish pupils and a decerebrate posture. Which one of the following is the MOST likely cause of her illness?

- ☐ A   Aspirin overdose
- ☐ B   Hepatitis A
- ☐ C   Hepatitis C
- ☐ D   Paracetamol overdose
- ☐ E   Wilson's disease

2.11 A 46-year-old woman is referred by a dermatologist to whom she presented with generalised itching. She was found to have the following biochemical results: bilirubin 50 mmol/l, ALP 270 iu/l, ALT 60 iu/l. Which one of the following is the MOST likely diagnosis?

- ☐ A   Alcoholic cirrhosis
- ☐ B   Chronic active hepatitis
- ☐ C   Haemachromatosis
- ☐ D   Primary biliary cirrhosis
- ☐ E   SLE

2.12 A 40-year-old alcoholic male presents to A&E with a history of upper abdominal pain radiating to his back accompanied by nausea and vomiting. He is shocked and mildly pyrexial. Which one of the following is the MOST likely diagnosis?

☐ A Acute cholecystitis

☐ B Acute pancreatitis

☐ C Alcoholic hepatitis

☐ D Opiate withdrawal

☐ E Perforated duodenal ulcer

2.13 A 36-year-old alcoholic presents with shock due to bleeding oesophageal varices. After resuscitation, which one of the following is the treatment of choice?

☐ A i.v. octreotide

☐ B i.v. glypressin

☐ C Oesophageal variceal endoscopic ligation

☐ D Oesophageal variceal sclerotherapy

☐ E TIPSS

2.14 A 30-year-old woman with chronic Crohn's disease of the colon is planning to have a child. She has required 2–3 courses of steroid each year for the last five years. Which one of the following should be offered to her?

☐ A Azathioprine

☐ B Continuous oral prednisolone

☐ C Cyclosporin

☐ D Infliximab

☐ E Methotrexate

2.15 **A 30-year-old gay man is referred by his GP after liver function tests. The patient presented with a vague flu-like illness, but was noted to be icteric. His LFTs were as follows: bilirubin 50 mmol/l, ALP 90 iu/l, ALT 35 iu/l. Which one of the following is the MOST likely diagnosis?**

- ☐ A Acute hepatitis A
- ☐ B Chronic hepatitis B
- ☐ C Hepatitis C
- ☐ D HIV hepatitis
- ☐ E Gilbert's syndrome

2.16 **A 70-year-old man presents with dysphagia. For 30 years he has experienced regular episodes of heartburn. An endoscopic biopsy shows Barrett's oesophagus with high grade dysplasia. Which one of the following would you use to treat this patient?**

- ☐ A Antireflux surgery
- ☐ B Laser ablation
- ☐ C Oesophagectomy
- ☐ D PPI treatment with repeat endoscopy in 3–6 months
- ☐ E Proton pump inhibitor alone

2.17 **A 46-year-old woman presents with rectal bleeding. She reports that she has had difficult defaecation for some years and has had to strain to pass her stools which are hard. The blood she has observed coats or follows her stool, rather than being mixed with it. Sigmoidoscopy reveals a raised ulcerated lesion on the anterior wall of the lower rectum. Which one of the following is the MOST likely diagnosis?**

- ☐ A Crohn's disease
- ☐ B Haemorrhoids
- ☐ C Lymphogranuloma venereum
- ☐ D Rectal carcinoma
- ☐ E Solitary rectal ulcer

2.18   A 70-year-old former POW with COPD presents with a two-month history of rectal bleeding and diarrhoea. On examination he has a hyperinflated chest with widespread wheeze. Sigmoidoscopy shows multiple polypoid lesions in the rectum. Which one of the following is the most likely diagnosis?

    ☐ A   Antibiotic diarrhoea

    ☐ B   Familial adenomatous polyposis

    ☐ C   Pneumatosis coli

    ☐ D   Schistosomiasis

    ☐ E   Villous rectal cancer

2.19   A 36-year-old presents with painless rectal bleeding. He is a gay man and has had several sexual relationships in the months prior to his symptoms. There are no signs on physical examination except on sigmoidoscopy, which shows a florid proctitis. Biopsies show inclusion bodies in the mucosa. Which one of the following is the correct diagnosis?

    ☐ A   CMV proctitis

    ☐ B   Herpes

    ☐ C   LGV

    ☐ D   Solitary rectal ulcer

    ☐ E   Syphilis

2.20   A 20-year-old man presents with massive haematemesis. He drinks little alcohol and does not inject drugs. His past medical history is unremarkable except for a prolonged stay on SCBU after being born prematurely. His spleen is palpable, but he has no stigmata of chronic liver disease. Which one of the following is the underlying diagnosis?

    ☐ A   Cirrhosis secondary to hepatitis C

    ☐ B   Cryptogenic cirrhosis

    ☐ C   Lymphoma

    ☐ D   Portal vein thrombosis

    ☐ E   Primary biliary cirrhosis

2.21 A 60-year-old Welsh sheep farmer is admitted for routine hip replacement surgery. On examination he is noted to have hepatomegaly. Ultrasonography reveals multiple cyst lesions with echogenic areas within the cysts. Which one of the following is the most likely diagnosis?

- ☐ A Haemangioma
- ☐ B Hydatid disease
- ☐ C Necrotic metastases
- ☐ D Polycystic disease
- ☐ E Simple hepatic cysts

2.22 A 66-year-old man reports a six-month history of diarrhoea. He has had diabetes for 10 months. Dietary measures were inadequate, so his GP prescribed escalating doses of metformin. Which one of the following is the cause of his diarrhoea?

- ☐ A Bacterial overgrowth
- ☐ B Bile salt diarrhoea
- ☐ C Chronic pancreatitis
- ☐ D IBS due to concerns about ill health
- ☐ E Metformin

2.23 One week after a colectomy with ileostomy for Crohn's disease, a 26-year-old woman begins to experience stomal diarrhoea. The pain around her stoma had started to settle, but increased again. Investigations show her CRP to have risen and her albumin to have fallen. Which one of the following is the cause of her problem?

- ☐ A Antibiotic diarrhoea
- ☐ B Bile salt diarrhoea
- ☐ C Functional diarrhoea due to her disquiet about her stoma
- ☐ D Recurrent Crohn's disease
- ☐ E Peristomal abscess

2.24 A 32-year-old man with dysphagia is found to have a hypertonic lower oesophageal sphincter with no peristalsis in the body of the oesophagus. Which one of the following is the treatment of choice?

- ☐ A Antireflux surgery
- ☐ B Botulinum toxin injection
- ☐ C Heller's myotomy
- ☐ D Domperidone
- ☐ E PPI therapy

2.25 After eating a very large Sunday lunch, a 42-year-old man vomits several times before experiencing severe chest pain. On presentation to A&E, he is shocked. His ECG is normal, but his CXR shows some shadowing in the left lower zone. Which one of the following is the diagnosis?

- ☐ A Boerhaave's syndrome
- ☐ B Gastritis
- ☐ C Mallory-Weiss tear
- ☐ D Myocardial infarction
- ☐ E Oesophagitis

GASTROENTEROLOGY: MULTIPLE CHOICE QUESTIONS

Mark your answers with a tick (True) or a cross (False) in the box provided.

2.26 The hormone gastrin

☐ A is the main stimulus for acid secretion

☐ B has a plasma half-life of one hour

☐ C exerts its acid secretory effects by direct action on the parietal cell

☐ D has trophic effects on gastric mucosal endocrine cells

☐ E is found only in G cells of the gastric antrum

2.27 In primary biliary cirrhosis

☐ A positive antimitochondrial antibodies occur in over 95% ofpatients

☐ B pruritus may be the only clinical feature

☐ C centri-zonal necrosis is characteristic on liver biopsy

☐ D liver copper is increased

☐ E there is an association with Sjögren's syndrome

2.28 Following a large paracetamol overdose

☐ A the serum albumin is a reliable indicator of the severity of liver injury

☐ B alkalosis is a common feature

☐ C a prothrombin time of >100 seconds requires immediate treatment with vitamin K

☐ D liver transplantation should be considered when the serum bilirubin is >100 mmol/l

☐ E intravenous N-acetyl cysteine is the treatment of choice

2.29 Pernicious anaemia

☐ A is associated with gastric carcinoid tumours

☐ B is best diagnosed by positive intrinsic factor antibodies

☐ C is always associated with chronic atrophic gastritis

☐ D patients require regular endoscopic surveillance

☐ E is associated with an increased risk of carcinoma of the oesophagus

2.30 Bleeding oesophageal varices

- ☐ A may occur in the absence of cirrhosis
- ☐ B prognosis depends on the severity of the underlying liver disease
- ☐ C can be treated by transjugular intrahepatic portosystemic shunting
- ☐ D require immediate endoscopy and sclerotherapy
- ☐ E rarely respond to octreotide

2.31 In colorectal cancer

- ☐ A there is a correlation between the consumption of meat and animal fat and the likelihood of developing colon cancer
- ☐ B faecal occult blood testing will detect 90% of cases
- ☐ C there is an increased incidence of rectal tumours in patients who abstain from alcohol consumption
- ☐ D the adenomatous polyposis coli (APC) gene maps to chromosome 2
- ☐ E hereditary non-polyposis colon cancer accounts for up to a third of all cases of colon cancer

2.32 Recognised gastrointestinal infections in AIDS include

- ☐ A cytomegalovirus
- ☐ B *Cryptococcus neoformans*
- ☐ C herpes simplex virus
- ☐ D *Pneumocystis carinii*
- ☐ E atypical mycobacteria

2.33 *Helicobacter pylori*

- ☐ A is a Gram-positive spirochaete
- ☐ B has a prevalence that decreases with age
- ☐ C is associated with gastric carcinoma
- ☐ D can be diagnosed by a hydrogen breath test
- ☐ E produces the enzyme urease

2.34   Coeliac disease

- ☐ A is associated with HLA B12
- ☐ B is characterised by increased polymorphs in the lamina propria
- ☐ C is a cause of reversible male infertility
- ☐ D produces reduced small intestinal villus and crypt length
- ☐ E is associated with epilepsy

2.35   Pseudomembranous colitis

- ☐ A typically spares the rectum
- ☐ B may occur after treatment with metronidazole
- ☐ C is caused by toxin-producing *Clostridium difficile*
- ☐ D is best treated with intravenous vancomycin
- ☐ E relapse is very uncommon after treatment

2.36   Chronic pancreatitis

- ☐ A may be caused by hypercalcaemia
- ☐ B rarely produces biliary strictures
- ☐ C is associated with peripheral vascular disease
- ☐ D may cause portal hypertension
- ☐ E is usually painless

2.37   Folic acid

- ☐ A is absorbed predominantly in the jejunum
- ☐ B blood levels are reduced in stagnant loop syndrome
- ☐ C bioavailability is impaired by cooking
- ☐ D body stores are adequate for 3 years
- ☐ E is effective treatment for alcohol-induced macrocytosis

2.38   The following are features of hepatic encephalopathy without coma:

- ☐ A inversion of normal sleep pattern
- ☐ B hyporeflexia
- ☐ C decreased muscle tone
- ☐ D constructional apraxia
- ☐ E absent pupillary response

2.39   The solitary rectal ulcer syndrome

☐ A is common in homosexual men

☐ B may cause iron deficiency anaemia

☐ C is associated with laxative abuse

☐ D usually involves an ulcer on the posterior rectal wall

☐ E commonly causes perineal pain

2.40   Cholecystokinin

☐ A relaxes smooth muscle

☐ B delays gastric emptying

☐ C stimulates gastric acid output

☐ D stimulates pancreatic exocrine secretion

☐ E increases appetite

2.41   The irritable bowel syndrome

☐ A is associated with disordered REM sleep

☐ B can be precipitated by travellers' diarrhoea

☐ C is characterised by visceral hypersensitivity

☐ D is associated with dysmenorrhoea

☐ E is characterised by rapid small intestinal transit

2.42   Wilson's disease is associated with

☐ A isolated psychiatric illness

☐ B increased biliary copper excretion

☐ C cerebellar ataxia

☐ D decreased serum caeruloplasmin

☐ E copper deposits in Descemet's membrane

2.43   Bilirubin

☐ A is entirely formed from haemoglobin breakdown

☐ B is transported in the blood bound to serum albumin before liver conjugation

☐ C is predominantly conjugated in the blood of normal subjects

☐ D is water soluble when conjugated

☐ E is metabolised to urobilinogen by gut bacterial action

2.44   Gastrointestinal manifestations of mutations of the *c-ret* oncogene include

☐ A sporadic gastric carcinoid tumours

☐ B Zollinger-Ellison syndrome

☐ C Hirschsprung's disease

☐ D cystic fibrosis

☐ E haemochromatosis

2.45   Gastro-oesophageal reflux

☐ A is characterised by increased oesophageal clearance

☐ B is best diagnosed by endoscopy

☐ C is most effectively treated by H_2-antagonists

☐ D occurs commonly in systemic sclerosis

☐ E rarely produces odynophagia

2.46   Systemic sclerosis of the gastrointestinal tract

☐ A most commonly affects the oesophagus

☐ B is associated with primary biliary cirrhosis

☐ C causes narrowing of the small intestinal lumen

☐ D may produce diarrhoea responding to antibiotic therapy

☐ E is a recognised cause of steatorrhoea

2.47 Dietary fat

☐ A is ingested primarily as cholesterol

☐ B can only be absorbed as free fatty acid

☐ C stimulates cholecystokinin release from the small intestine

☐ D absorption is enhanced by bile salts

☐ E decreases small intestinal transit time

2.48 Mesalazine compounds

☐ A are useful in the maintenance of remission of ulcerative colitis

☐ B have no value in the treatment of active small bowel Crohn's disease

☐ C are contraindicated in pregnancy

☐ D may cause impotence

☐ E can be given by enema

2.49 Delayed gastric emptying

☐ A occurs in hyperglycaemia

☐ B is characteristic of functional dyspepsia

☐ C may be treated with erythromycin

☐ D may be caused by anti-Parkinsonian drugs

☐ E is a feature of the dumping syndrome

2.50 *Clostridium difficile*

☐ A produces a cytopathic toxin detectable in >90% of patients with pseudomembranous colitis

☐ B is part of the normal colonic flora in 15% of healthy adults

☐ C is the cause of up to a third of all cases of antibiotic related diarrhoea

☐ D is best treated with intravenous vancomycin

☐ E may cause toxic dilatation of the colon

NEPHROLOGY

'Best of Five'

Helen Paynter MRCP
Staff Grade Renal Medicine
Gloucestershire Royal Hospital
Gloucester

MCQs

Philip A Kalra MA MB Chir FRCP MD
Consultant Nephrologist and Honorary Lecturer
Hope Hospital
Salford Royal Hospitals Trust
and University of Manchester

NEPHROLOGY: 'BEST OF FIVE' QUESTIONS

For each of the questions select the ONE most appropriate answer from the options provided.

3.1   Which one of the following is true with regard to cholesterol embolisation?

☐ A   It is a rare cause of renal damage

☐ B   It is best diagnosed by arteriography

☐ C   It is often associated with blue mottling of the hands

☐ D   It is usually manifest by loin pain and frank haematuria

☐ E   It is often associated with eosinophilia

3.2   Which one of the following is true of hepatitis C infection with regard to the kidney?

☐ A   Membranous glomerulonephritis is typical

☐ B   Pulsed methylprednisolone may be used in treatment

☐ C   Renal remission is rare

☐ D   The disease is mediated by cold agglutinins

☐ E   There is direct viral infection of the glomerular endothelium

3.3   Which one of the following is typical of a renal biopsy in a patient with diabetic nephropathy?

☐ A   Diffuse glomerular capillary thickening and basement membrane spikes

☐ B   Green birefringence on staining with Congo Red

☐ C   Intracapillary hyaline thrombi

☐ D   Mesangial hypercellularity and fibrinoid necrosis

☐ E   Mesangial widening, basement membrane thickening and capillary obliteration

3.4   Which one of the following is characteristic of vitamin D resistant rickets?

☐ A   Elevated 1, 25 dihydroxycholecalciferol

☐ B   Expression confined to males

☐ C   Glycosuria

☐ D   Impaired phosphate excretion

☐ E   Normal PTH levels

3.5 **Which one of the following is true of the complications of renal transplantation?**

- [ ] A CMV matching of donor and recipient is essential
- [ ] B Gastric ulceration is partly attributable to increased rate of *Helicobacter pylori* carriage
- [ ] C Pneumocystis typically occurs at around one year post transplant
- [ ] D Reverse barrier nursing for ten days after surgery is mandatory
- [ ] E The major cause of mortality is malignancy

3.6 **Which one of the following is true for most patients with moderate chronic renal impairment?**

- [ ] A Alcohol is contraindicated
- [ ] B Dairy products are a useful source of calcium
- [ ] C Fluid intake should be 2 to 3 litres per day
- [ ] D The diet should be high in cholesterol
- [ ] E Very low protein diet is beneficial

3.7 **In the treatment of poisoning which one of the following is true?**

- [ ] A Haemodialysis following death cap mushroom ingestion does not affect mortality despite good toxin removal
- [ ] B Haemodialysis is ineffective for salicylate poisoning if coma and acute renal failure have ensued
- [ ] C Haemodialysis is useful for amitriptyline poisoning
- [ ] D Peritoneal dialysis is generally preferable to haemodialysis
- [ ] E Use of bicarbonate as a dialysate buffer is contraindicated

3.8 **Which one of the following is true of renal involvement in HIV infection?**

- [ ] A Antiviral therapy is of little benefit in HIV-associated nephropathy
- [ ] B HIV-associated nephropathy is indistinguishable histologically from focal segmental glomerulosclerosis
- [ ] C HIV-associated nephropathy typically presents with nephrotic range proteinuria
- [ ] D Hypernatraemia is common in HIV infection
- [ ] E Renal involvement is common in AIDS

3.9 **Which one of the following is therapeutically useful in cystinuria?**

☐ A Allopurinol

☐ B Cysteamine

☐ C Desferrioxamine

☐ D Penicillamine

☐ E Potassium citrate

3.10 **Which one of the following is NOT used in the treatment of renal stone disease?**

☐ A Bendrofluazide

☐ B Cholestyramine

☐ C Ibuprofen

☐ D Prednisolone

☐ E Pyridoxine

3.11 **A 24-year-old known epileptic is admitted to casualty in status epilepticus. He is treated with intravenous phenytoin. 48 hours later he is found to have acute renal failure. Blood results are as follows: potassium 7.1 mmol/l, creatinine 782 μmol/l, corrected calcium 1.9 mmol/l, phosphate 3.1 mmol/l. What simple procedure would be most useful diagnostically?**

☐ A BM stix

☐ B Electrocardiogram

☐ C Fundoscopy

☐ D Plain abdominal X-ray

☐ E Urine dipstick and microscopy

3.12 **Which one of the following is NOT typically associated with reduced serum complement activity?**

☐ A Acute post-streptococcal nephritis

☐ B Antiglomerular basement membrane disease

☐ C Essential mixed cryoglobulinaemia

☐ D Lupus nephritis

☐ E Type II mesangiocapillary glomerulonephritis

3.13 **Which one of the following examination findings in a patient with renal disease is likely to be helpful in determining the aetiology of the condition described?**

   ☐ A   Adenoma sebaceum in a patient with microscopic haematuria

   ☐ B   Grade II hypertensive retinopathy in a patient presenting with creatinine of 647 μmol/l

   ☐ C   Hot, tender, swollen leg in a patient with proteinuria 7 g/24 hours

   ☐ D   Partial lipodystrophy in a patient with a creatinine of 150 μmol/l and normal urinary sediment

   ☐ E   Truncal obesity, thin skin and striae in a patient with a creatinine of 270 μmol/l and proteinuria 1.5 g/24 hours

3.14 **Which one of the following features would make a diagnosis of poststreptococcal glomerulonephritis unlikely?**

   ☐ A   Infection 2 weeks ago with an alpha haemolytic streptococcus

   ☐ B   Patient is a 7-year-old female

   ☐ C   Proteinuria 1.1 g/24 hours

   ☐ D   No elevation of antistreptolysin titre

   ☐ E   No impairment of renal function at presentation

3.15 **Which one of the following is true with regard to blood pressure and pregnancy?**

   ☐ A   Eclampsia can occur without previous hypertension

   ☐ B   It is important to use Korotkoff phase V for blood pressure measurement

   ☐ C   The accepted threshold for physiological proteinuria is 0.8 g/24 hr

   ☐ D   The physiological fall in blood pressure is due to reduced cardiac work

   ☐ E   The risk of pre-eclampsia increases with each subsequent pregnancy

3.16 **Which one of the following is true with regard to the management of renal osteodystrophy?**

☐ A A high cheese diet is a useful way of increasing calcium intake

☐ B Phosphate binders must be taken on an empty stomach

☐ C Severe hyperphosphataemia is a contraindication to the administration of 1, 25 hydroxyvitamin D

☐ D Surgical removal of severely enlarged glands is often necessary in secondary hyperparathyroidism

☐ E The desferrioxamine stimulation test is useful to diagnose iron overload

3.17 **Which one of the following is true with regard to proteinuria?**

☐ A A urinary protein excretion of 3 g/l, in conjunction with microscopic haematuria, may be attributable to strenuous exercise

☐ B In orthostatic proteinuria, the proteinuria is only present during recumbency

☐ C Membranous glomerulonephritis is a major cause of the nephrotic syndrome in young adults

☐ D Microalbuminuria is diagnosed by Albustix testing

☐ E Pathological proteinuria is pathognomonic of glomerular pathology

3.18 **Which one of the following patients is least likely to develop clinically evident diabetic nephropathy within the next year?**

☐ A A 43-year-old man who has had Type 1 DM for 11 years, and who has early retinopathy

☐ B A 50-year-old woman with no past medical history, found on routine testing to have glycosuria +++

☐ C A 60-year-old man who developed Type 1 DM 43 years ago

☐ D A Caucasian subject 17 years after development of Type 2 DM

☐ E A Japanese subject 17 years after development of Type 2 DM

3.19 **Which one of the following is NOT a common feature of the acute phase of haemolytic uraemic syndrome (HUS)?**

☐ A Hypercalcaemia

☐ B Hyponatraemia

☐ C Neutrophilia

☐ D Reticulocytosis

☐ E Thrombocytopenia

3.20 **Which one of the following is NOT a contraindication to peritoneal dialysis?**

☐ A Acute renal failure in childhood

☐ B Chronic obstructive airways disease

☐ C Recent surgery for abdominal aortic aneurysm

☐ D Salicylate poisoning

☐ E Severe malnutrition

3.21 **In a healthy man, on a normal diet of 70 g protein and 4 g sodium each day, which one of the following is untrue?**

☐ A The minimum required water intake is approximately 1.35 l/day

☐ B The net insensible water loss is approximately 0.2 l/day

☐ C The obligated urine volume is approximately 0.8 l/day

☐ D Water intake of 10 litres in one day would not result in hyponatraemia

☐ E Water loss in stools is less than 0.05 l/day

3.22 **Which one of the following is the most important cause of death among UK patients with end-stage renal failure?**

☐ A Cardiac/vascular

☐ B Complications of transplantation

☐ C Infection

☐ D Malignancy

☐ E Voluntary withdrawal of dialysis/suicide

3.23   **Which one of the following statements concerning haematuria is untrue?**

☐   A   A high proportion of distorted red cells suggests a glomerular origin

☐   B   Family history may be relevant

☐   C   Haematuria is visible at a concentration of approximately 5 ml blood per litre of urine

☐   D   Haematuria rarely results from standard warfarinisation in the absence of structural lesions

☐   E   1 g/day proteinuria would be expected with haematuria due to a bladder malignancy

3.24   **Which one of the following is likely to be therapeutically useful in a patient suffering from hepatorenal syndrome?**

☐   A   Angiotensin converting enzyme inhibition

☐   B   Combined liver and kidney transplantation

☐   C   Continuous arterio-venous haemofiltration

☐   D   Correction of hyponatraemia with normal saline infusion

☐   E   Volume expansion with colloid

3.25   **In the investigation of a neonate with renal cysts, which one of the following is MOST likely to allow differentiation between autosomal recessive and autosomal dominant polycystic disease?**

☐   A   Intravenous pyelogram of patient

☐   B   Liver ultrasonography of patient

☐   C   Renal biopsy of patient

☐   D   Renal ultrasonography of patient

☐   E   Renal ultrasonography of teenage parents

NEPHROLOGY: MULTIPLE CHOICE QUESTIONS

Mark your answers with a tick (True) or a cross (False) in the box provided.

3.26   The following can cause acute renal failure in overdose:

☐ A   paracetamol

☐ B   paraquat

☐ C   indomethacin

☐ D   ethylene glycol

☐ E   iron

3.27   Useful measurements to distinguish between acute renal failure and chronic renal failure include

☐ A   sodium level in urine

☐ B   ultrasound scan of kidneys to assess size

☐ C   serum phosphate

☐ D   presence of left ventricular hypertrophy on ECG

☐ E   hypokalaemia

3.28   Characteristics of the hepatorenal syndrome include

☐ A   intratubular deposition of bilirubin

☐ B   oliguria

☐ C   daily urinary sodium losses exceeding 50 mmol

☐ D   good prognosis following renal transplantation

☐ E   diuresis following albumin infusion

3.29   In patients with acute renal failure

☐ A   eosinophilia and hypocomplementaemia are typical of allergic interstitial nephritis

☐ B   non-oliguria indicates a better prognosis

☐ C   dopamine typically causes diuresis

☐ D   renal obstruction is excluded by polyuria

☐ E   aminoglycosides are always contraindicated and should be avoided if at all possible

3.30 **In the normal kidney**

☐ A maximal tubular re-absorption of phosphate can be increased physiologically

☐ B tubular re-absorption of phosphate can be increased by PTH

☐ C in chronic acidosis the excretion of ammonium in the urine is greater than in acute acidosis

☐ D alkalosis leads to decreased secretion of potassium

☐ E acetazolamide leads to decreased distal secretion of potassium

3.31 **Renal excretion of water is increased in association with**

☐ A hyperkalaemia

☐ B hypokalaemia

☐ C recovery phase of ATN

☐ D hyperaldosteronism

☐ E chronic renal failure

3.32 **Filtration at the glomerulus**

☐ A results from a net filtration pressure of 10 mmHg in normal subjects

☐ B is favoured if a molecule is positively charged

☐ C results in a filtration fraction of 40% in normal subjects

☐ D results in the formation of approximately 360 litres of filtrate per day in normal man

☐ E is reduced by efferent arteriolar constriction

3.33 **Concerning the renal function at 36 weeks of pregnancy**

☐ A a serum creatinine of 150 μmol/l requires investigation

☐ B a urea of 1 mmol/l is due to malnutrition

☐ C there is a reduced glomerular filtration rate

☐ D the serum magnesium concentration is typically low

☐ E uric acid levels are characteristically high

3.34   The clearance

    ☐   A   of a substance by the kidney is defined as the volume of blood cleared of that substance in one minute

    ☐   B   of a compound which is freely filtered by the kidney and neither secreted nor reabsorbed is a measure of the renal plasma flow

    ☐   C   of inulin is normal when plasma inulin = 0.02 mg/ml, urinary inulin = 2.5 mg/ml, and the urinary flow rate = 60 ml/hr

    ☐   D   of urea is an accurate estimate of the glomerular filtration rate (GMR) in the hydrated state

    ☐   E   of penicillin is reduced by probenecid

3.35   The following will result in an increase in urinary sodium excretion:

    ☐   A   a decrease in renal sympathetic nervous activity

    ☐   B   a rise of 15 mm Hg in renal arterial pressure

    ☐   C   a 10% increase in glomerular filtration rate (GFR)

    ☐   D   a decrease in the plasma protein concentration

    ☐   E   an increase in venous volume

3.36   Ascent to 10,000 ft can lead to a reduction in arterial pCO_2 in normal people. The response in the kidney

    ☐   A   leads to a fall in plasma $[HCO_3]^-$

    ☐   B   is corrective rather than compensatory

    ☐   C   results in arterial pCO_2 returning to normal

    ☐   D   leads to a fall in plasma pH

    ☐   E   occurs predominantly in the proximal tubules

3.37   Renin

    ☐   A   is released from the cells of the macula densa in response to sodium depletion

    ☐   B   release is stimulated by renal sympathetic nervous stimulation

    ☐   C   increases in response to cortical ischaemia

    ☐   D   leads to the production of a plasma borne vasoconstrictor

    ☐   E   leads to an increase in thirst

3.38   Relative contraindications to continuous ambulatory peritoneal dialysis (CAPD) include

- ☐ A   obesity
- ☐ B   rheumatoid arthritis
- ☐ C   previous appendicectomy
- ☐ D   chronic obstructive airways disease
- ☐ E   cardiac failure

3.39   Indications for urgent dialysis in uraemic patients include

- ☐ A   asterixis
- ☐ B   itching
- ☐ C   pericarditis
- ☐ D   peripheral neuropathy
- ☐ E   hiccoughing

3.40   A man of 40 is found to be uraemic. The following facts might give a useful lead to the aetiology:

- ☐ A   he had haematuria in childhood
- ☐ B   he works in an iron foundry
- ☐ C   three of his children had haemolytic disease of the newborn
- ☐ D   he has tablets regularly for fibrositis
- ☐ E   he suffers from migraine

3.41   In moderate (not end stage) chronic renal failure

- ☐ A   the level of blood insulin is inappropriately high compared with the level of blood glucose
- ☐ B   the main cause of growth failure is growth hormone deficiency
- ☐ C   polyuria is more common than oliguria
- ☐ D   typically there is hypercalciuria
- ☐ E   treatment and control of hypertension will improve the glomerular filtration rate

3.42   When imaging the renal tract of uraemic subjects

☐ A   renal obstruction is best diagnosed by static radionuclide scanning

☐ B   dehydration is indicated to improve the quality of intravenous urograms

☐ C   lateral displacement of the ureters is characteristic of retroperitoneal fibrosis

☐ D   large kidneys exclude a diagnosis of chronic renal failure

☐ E   coarse kidney scarring is diagnostic of reflux nephropathy

3.43   Membranous glomerulonephritis

☐ A   is characterised by highly selective proteinuria

☐ B   usually leads to end-stage renal failure within 2 years

☐ C   is characterised by IgG deposits within the basement membrane

☐ D   commonly presents with the nephritic syndrome

☐ E   is associated with malignancy

3.44   IgA nephropathy

☐ A   is the most common form of glomerulonephritis

☐ B   is complicated by end-stage renal failure in over 50% of those affected

☐ C   may show glomerular crescents during episodes of macroscopic haematuria

☐ D   causes loin pain owing to bleeding from peripheral renal arteries

☐ E   has a worse prognosis when proteinuria exceeds 1 g/day

3.45   Renal vein thrombosis is a complication of

☐ A   renal carcinoma

☐ B   gastroenteritis in childhood

☐ C   renal amyloidosis

☐ D   IgA glomerulonephritis

☐ E   pyelonephritis

3.46 **The following are genetically-transmitted diseases that may involve the kidney:**

☐ A   von Hippel-Lindau syndrome

☐ B   cystinosis

☐ C   vesico-ureteric reflux

☐ D   Noonan's syndrome

☐ E   systematic lupus erythematosus

3.47 **Concerning vesico-ureteric reflux**

☐ A   it may remain clinically silent until adulthood

☐ B   it may present with nausea and vomiting

☐ C   it is usually associated with coliform urinary tract infection

☐ D   ureteric reimplantation is of no value

☐ E   the prophylactic antibiotic of choice is ampicillin

3.48 **Active tuberculosis of the urinary tract**

☐ A   is a recognised cause of renal calculi

☐ B   may cause ureteric obstruction when treated

☐ C   is a contraindication to renal transplantation

☐ D   is a recognised cause of urge incontinence

☐ E   is associated with a normal chest X-ray in over 50% of cases

3.49 **In distal (type 1) renal tubular acidosis**

☐ A   there is reduced ammonia formation despite good glomerular filtration rate

☐ B   the urine pH cannot be below 7.0

☐ C   there is an association with renal calcification

☐ D   there is hypokalaemia

☐ E   the condition only occurs in children

3.50 **The following drugs may be harmful in patients with chronic renal failure:**

☐ A oxytetracycline

☐ B mesalazine

☐ C omeprazole

☐ D felodipine

☐ E ibuprofen

ENDOCRINOLOGY: 'BEST OF FIVE' ANSWERS

1.1   D: Withhold any antithyroid treatment and repeat thyroid function testing in 3 weeks

Thyrotoxicosis presenting in pregnancy is due either to Graves' disease or cross-reactive activation of the TSH receptor by the very high HCG levels in the first trimester of pregnancy (the two hormones have a common alpha subunit). Characteristics of the latter condition are that it is commonly associated with hyperemesis gravidarum, occurs in the first trimester and subsides spontaneously in the subsequent weeks (as the HCG level falls), is biochemically mild and is more frequently seen with twin or molar pregnancies. A confident diagnosis cannot be made in the absence of Graves' eye disease and a wait-and-see policy is appropriate if the degree of thyrotoxicosis is mild and the patient clinically well. Propylthiouracil may be used and is safe but is often unnecessary. Radio-nucleotide scans are contraindicated in pregnancy and subtotal thyroidectomy is only indicated in Graves' disease with ongoing thyrotoxicosis in patients intolerant of medication. There are no grounds for advising termination except in a molar pregnancy.

1.2   E: Short synacthen testing followed by immediate treatment with hydrocortisone

External beam radiotherapy continues to cause pituitary damage for 20 years or more after treatment. It is most likely that this man has now developed pan hypopituitarism with secondary gonadal failure, but also adrenal failure (low Na^+ and tiredness but the K^+ is not raised as mineralocorticoid function is preserved in secondary adrenal failure) and possibly also secondary hypothyroidism (the TSH is often misleadingly normal but T4 or T3 testing shows a very low value). The most dangerous element here is adrenal failure. Insulin stress testing or treatment with thyroxine (which accelerates metabolism of adrenal steroids) may precipitate a fatal hypotensive crisis. Adrenal failure should be assumed. Short synacthen testing (with synthetic ACTH and cortisol sampling at 0, 30 and 60 mins) is safe and if immediately available involves minimal delay. Alternatively a sample for random cortisol could be saved prior to urgent treatment with parenteral hydrocortisone. Thyroxine and testosterone replacement can be commenced later.

1.3   D: Corticosteroids act more slowly because they act via modulating gene transcription

Beta agonists like adrenaline act via cell surface 7-transmembrane receptors and once bound to their ligand activate G proteins that in turn activate the enzyme adenylcyclase. The result is rapid (seconds) generation of cyclic AMP which acts as an intracellular second messenger to mediate the actions of the drug/hormone. Corticosteroids are lipid soluble but their effects are generated slowly because they act by modulating gene transcription and new proteins must either first be synthesised or existing ones be degraded. However, once generated, these changes in intracellular protein result in prolonged action beyond the serum half-life of the hormone.

1.4   C: A high renin level

Renal artery stenosis results in high renin and high aldosterone levels in contrast to Conn's syndrome in which the aldosterone is high but the renin is characteristically suppressed. While the aldosterone level is high in both cases, it will not discriminate between the two conditions.

1.5   E: 24-hour urinary free cortisol

To distinguish Cushing's syndrome from simple obesity, a 24-hour urinary free cortisol or an overnight low dose (1 mg) dexamethasone suppression test is typically used. There is loss of diurnal variation in cortisol in Cushing's syndrome. This means that the morning cortisol remains high, but a high evening (midnight) value is strongly suggestive of organic disease. Salivary cortisol measurements can be used to assess this but the assay is not routinely available. Serum potassium is low and bicarbonate high in Cushing's syndrome but these features would also be seen in hypertension treated with a diuretic and are not very specific for Cushing's syndrome. ACTH levels may be inappropriately 'normal' in pituitary dependent Cushing's. Adrenal or pituitary scanning may be abnormal in the aetiology of Cushing's but in the absence of a biochemical diagnosis, radiological abnormalities could be due to non-functioning 'incidentalomas' which are relatively common at both sights.

1.6   B: Basal bolus insulin

The DIGAMI study shows that diabetics treated with intravenous insulin for at least the first 24 hours followed by subcutaneous insulin for at least three months have significantly lower mortality rates up to 3.4 years later. This is regardless of the form of treatment they were taking prior to the MI. The mechanism of this is unclear but may be related to the reduction in free fatty acids released as part of the stress reaction. He has a degree of heart failure and renal impairment meaning that metformin is contraindicated because of the risk of lactic acidosis.

1.7   D: To reduce his insulin to maintain relatively high blood sugars (8–15 mmol/l) for at least 3 months

This individual has hypoglycaemia unawareness. This is relatively common in long-standing diabetics, particularly in individuals who have very tight blood sugar control and have frequent hypoglycaemic episodes. It appears that the recurrent hypos result in a blunting of the adrenaline (and glucagon) response to hypoglycaemia, making it harder for the individual to detect, take evasive action (eating) and avoid further hypos – hence the phrase 'hypos beget hypos'. A relaxation in diabetic control with reduced insulin doses for 3 months such that all hyopglycaemic episodes are avoided results in a restoration of hypoglycaemia awareness and is the most appropriate advice. While regular blood sugar testing may help, it is not sustainable in the long term and will not in itself restore hypoglycaemia awareness. Eating every 2 hours may reduce hypoglycaemic episodes but would result in weight gain and would not be the ideal way to manage this problem.

1.8   B: Aggressive management of hypertension

At the stage of microalbuminuria in diabetic nephropathy, glomerular filtration rates are relatively well preserved and serum creatinine is normal. Aggressive hypertension management down to levels as low as 130/80 has proved to be the best method of delaying decline in renal function and progression to macroalbuminuria. Good glycaemic control is key to preventing the development of nephropathy in the first place but plays a rather minor role in preventing progression from micro- to macroalbuminuria. Likewise, a low protein diet and aggressive lipid lowering can contribute to maintaining renal function but their role is limited. Diuretics are not contraindicated in diabetic nephropathy and can be used to treat hypertension.

1.9   D: Trans-sphenoidal surgery

The best chance of cure of small to moderate sized growth-hormone secreting pituitary tumours causing acromegaly is trans-sphenoidal surgery, with cure rates approaching 70% in experienced centres. With larger tumours, complete cure is unlikely, but it is still appropriate to debulk the tumour followed by radiotherapy. Octreotide therapy is very effective at lowering growth hormone levels by inhibiting growth hormone synthesis and release. However it is very expensive, has to be given parenterally at least monthly, does not effect a cure or cause much tumour shrinkage and its exact role in therapy remains to be defined. Only 20% of GH-secreting tumours respond to bromocriptine and yttrium implantation has now given way to the safer procedure of external beam radiotherapy via 3 overlapping fields.

1.10   C: Hydrocortisone 10 mg mane, 5 mg pm and fludrocortisone 100 μg mane

In primary adrenocortical failure (Addison's disease) both gluco- and mineralo-corticoid (e.g. fludrocortisone) replacement therapy is essential. The glucocorticoid treatment should be given at the lowest possible doses to avoid long-term hypercortisolaemia. Possible dosing for glucocorticoid replacement alone includes hydrocortisone 10 mg mane/5 mg pm, or 10 mg bd, prednisolone 5 mg or dexamethasone 0.5 mg. Higher doses of any other of these drugs, except in an emergency, is detrimental in the long term with Cushingoid side-effects. Dexamethasone has no mineralocorticoid effect and could precipitate an adrenal crisis if given alone.

1.11   C: Prophylactic thyroidectomy and regular screening for phaeochromocytoma

Multiple endocrine neoplasia (MEN) Type 2 comprises hypercalcaemia (hyper-parathyroidism) and two potentially fatal conditions: medullary thyroid cancer (MTC) and phaeochromocytoma. By the time MTC is detectable on thyroid imaging it is unlikely to be curable and patients positive on genetic testing are now being advised to have a prophylactic thyroidectomy, typically before the age of 10 years. Bilateral adrenalectomy is a more dangerous procedure and may miss extra-adrenal phaeochromocytomas. Hence routine adrenalectomy is not advised but urinary catecholamine secretion should be measured regularly (e.g. yearly) followed by imaging if the screen proves positive. Pituitary tumours are a feature of MEN1 not MEN2.

1.12   A: A benign course is very likely in such cases

Scattered dark (terminal–non vellous) facial hairs and an escutcheon (hair between the umbilicus and pubic area) are common in women, as is hair on the lower arms and legs. When associated with menstrual irregularity dating from soon after the menarche or early 20s, by far the most common diagnosis is polycystic ovary syndrome. Normal or slightly raised levels of testosterone are typically present and a benign course with a 'plateau' in hair growth in the mid-20s is to be expected. Hair on the upper back is unusual. Signs of virilisation comprise clitoromegaly, voice deepening, breast atrophy, and male pattern baldness and indicate very marked increases in androgen levels. In such situations and whenever the testosterone level is markedly raised (e.g. > 5 nmol/l), screening for adrenal and ovarian tumours is mandatory. Congenital adrenal hyperplasia is also a cause but is usually diagnosed in childhood.

1.13   B: He could be started on a sulphonylurea, taught to test his own capillary glucose levels and be reassessed in one month

This gentleman is relatively thin and young and is likely to have Type 1 diabetes. He will have some residual beta cell function (insulin production) and in older individuals this may persist for several months or years. Weight loss at presentation is strongly suggestive of Type 1 diabetes but does not always occur in this older age group. Urgent hospital admission is not necessary, as he is not ketotic or obviously unwell. However, he should be observed closely as his beta cell function may decline rapidly and dietary advice alone with review in three months is satisfactory for Type 2 diabetes. Metformin is not appropriate. Treatment with a sulphonylurea to augment insulin production seems reasonable in this case but the patient should be reviewed as soon as possible (e.g. in one month) in case it is proving ineffective or hypoglycaemia has been precipitated.

1.14   A: Amino acids are an increasingly important source of substrates for glucose synthesis

Liver glycogen supplies glucose in the first 12 hours of fasting but is rapidly used up. After this, amino acids are increasingly the source of glucose synthesis, as fatty acids cannot be converted to glucose. Glucagon levels rise within the first 12 hours of starvation and remain high. Mild ketonuria is often detectable in the first 24 hours of starvation as the low insulin levels result in fatty acid mobilisation.

1.15   D: Treatment should be begun with a 'statin'

Such a high level of cholesterol in a young person without elevated triglyceride levels strongly suggests heterozygous familial hypercholesterolaemia (LDL receptor defect). This is autosomal dominantly inherited and heterozygotes typically suffer myocardial infarction around the age of 40, consistent with this man's family history. Current treatment is with high doses of HMG-CoA reductase inhibitors. The addition of a fibrate or plasmapheresis is sometimes required. Excess alcohol and uncontrolled diabetes are typically associated with a mixed (raised cholesterol and triglyceride) hyperlipidaemia.

1.16   C: Hyperparathyroidism and malignancy account for 90% of cases

Asymptomatic hypercalcaemia in females in this age group is typically due to hyperparathyroidism. Further investigation, particularly parathyroid hormone estimation is required to rule out the possibility of malignancy (with bony metastases or parathyroid hormone related protein production). Malignancy and hyperparathyroidism account for 90% of cases of chronic hypercalcaemia. Alkaline phosphatase levels may be raised in both conditions. 'Normal' or raised parathyroid hormone levels in the presence of hypercalcaemia confirm the diagnosis of hyperparathyroidism. In asymptomatic patients with hyperparathyroidism the indications for parathyroidectomy are controversial but include calcium levels above 3.0 mmol/l, hypercalcaemic crisis and renal stones. Calcium levels are usually stable over many years and parathyroidectomy is frequently not required.

1.17   A: Can improve patients' mood

Growth hormone is increasingly being given to adults who have demonstrable deficiency, most commonly due to pituitary tumours. It may raise mood and energy levels, reduce fat and increase lean body mass, prevent osteoporosis and cause favourable lipid changes. Modern therapy is with genetically engineered GH and so carries no risk of CJD. Treatment should be monitored with IGF-1 levels, as the profile of GH itself after injection is unphysiologic.

1.18 B: Primary hyperparathyroidism

The hypercalcaemia of primary hyperparathyroidism results in polyuria and polydipsia and can result in renal calculi from the hypercalciuria. It can result in glucose intolerance whether the calcium is raised or not and this improves with decreasing the PTH level. Primary hyperparathyroidism is the commonest cause of hypercalcaemia in the community (malignancy is the commonest in the hospital setting).

Schmidt's syndrome is an association of type 1 diabetes, hypothyroidism, hypogonadism and Addison's disease. Abdominal pain can be a feature of the presentation of Addison's disease but this disease is associated with hypoglycaemia, not hyperglycaemia. In a non-diabetic subject severe infection like pyelonephritis can result in hypoglycaemia, not hyperglycaemia. Somatostatinomas are exceedingly rare and are associated with diabetes and steatorrhoea.

1.19 E: Sickle cell screen

Glycation of haemoglobin is a non-enzymatic process that can be artificially lowered where there is increased red cell turnover such as pregnancy, blood loss or haemolysis (thalassaemia and sickle cell anaemia including their traits). It can be overestimated as high levels of triglycerides or bilirubin can interfere with the assay. Finally it can be difficult to interpret if other compounds bind to the haemoglobin (opiate addiction, uraemia, alcoholism, high dose aspirin).

1.20 B: Captopril

'Captopril cough' is not infrequent with ACE inhibitors, being present in 7% of patients. It may be more common in women than in men. This side-effect does not occur with the angiotensin II inhibitors, as they do not inhibit bradykinin breakdown. ACE inhibitors have been felt to improve diabetic nephropathy in normotensive patients with type 1 diabetes; this is probably the case although the evidence is not complete. The commonest cause of death is macrovascular complications in type 2 diabetic patients. The important management issue is aggressive control of BP and the agent used is not important.

Beta-blockers can precipitate asthma which can occasionally present with dry cough without wheezing or shortness of breath but this is a less likely answer than captopril. Both doxazosin and nifedipine are usually very well tolerated though the former can be associated with postural hypotension on initiation of therapy.

1.21   D: Medullary thyroid carcinoma

Medullary thyroid carcinoma (MTC) can secrete a variety of peptides and prostaglandins resulting in extra thyroid symptoms. Diarrhoea and sweating are the most common. It is an important tumour to exclude since it can metastasise early and 20 year survival rates following treatment are as low as 44%. Though MTC is usually sporadic, it can be inherited as part of multiple endocrine neoplasia syndrome (MEN). MEN2a consists of MCT, hyperparathyroidism and phaeochromocytoma, and MEN2b consists of MCT, phaeochromocytoma and mucosal neuromas. Both types are transmitted in an autosomal dominant fashion.

Acromegaly can also cause sweating, in this case due to sweat gland hypertrophy, but usually not diarrhoea. Cushing's disease also rarely presents with these symptoms. Both these conditions also rarely show such strong family history. Other causes of sweating to remember for the exam are phaeochromocytoma and carcinoid syndrome which are investigated for by measuring urinary excretion of vanillymandelic acid and 5-hydroxyindoleacetic acid, respectively.

1.22   D: Subacute thyroiditis

Subacute thyroiditis classically presents with a painful, tender thyroid gland which feels hard because of the inflammatory infiltrate. There is a phase of thyrotoxicosis with increased secretion of T4 and T3 and a suppressed TSH. It is associated with a raised ESR. Thyroid radioiodine uptake scan shows low uptake due to the inability of the damaged thyroid epithelium to take up iodine. There is then a transitory euthyroid phase which may follow on to a hypothyroid phase. Depending on the amount of damage to the thyroid gland the hypothyroid phase is variable but can last for months and may be permanent (5% of cases). Antithyroid drugs are ineffective and treatment consists of analgesia and if symptoms are severe prednisolone.

Biochemical hyperthyroidism followed by hypothyroidism is also seen in post partum thyroiditis though in this case, there is no neck pain and the ESR is normal. They are more likely to be positive for thyroid auto-antibodies both before and after presentation, whereas in subacute thyroiditis there tends to be a transient rise in auto-antibodies.

1.23   C: Metformin

Metformin is the first choice, as it does not increase appetite like a sulphonylurea. It decreases gluconeogenesis and increases glucose utilisation and improves insulin sensitivity. It is contraindicated in renal or liver failure as it can predispose to lactic acidosis. Phenformin is not licensed in the UK. Acarbose has a lot of gastrointestinal side-effects and poor glucose lowering effects. Rosiglitazone is a new class of thiozolidinediones licensed in the UK for dual therapy with either a biguanide or sulphonlyurea i.e. not on its own and not with insulin.

1.24   D: A moderately raised LH level and a positive withdrawal bleed following *Provera* **challenge**

The typical endocrine changes in polycystic ovarian syndrome are a raised LH/FSH ratio with the FSH in the normal range, a normal or mildly raised prolactin, a mildly raised testosterone and a positive (withdrawal bleed present) response to *Provera* challenge. This last is because although the cycles are anovulatory, the ovary still makes oestrogen in amounts sufficient to prevent osteoporosis and oestrogenise the uterus. High FSH levels are typically seen in primary ovarian failure and a suppressed LH/FSH level with a raised prolactin suggests that hyperprolactinaemia is the primary cause of the amenorrhoea (e.g. due to a prolactin microadenoma).

1.25   D: Replace gliclazide with basal bolus insulin

There are a few studies using sulphonylureas in pregnancy, but accepted practice presently is to convert all pregnant women with diabetes on oral hypoglycaemic agents to insulin as soon as they are known to be pregnant. Gliclazide can cross the placenta and there is a risk of fetal hypoglycaemia. In addition, diabetic control should be immaculate in order to avoid congenital abnormalities, macrosomia or fetal loss. The best way of achieving this would be with a basal bolus regime with three injections of a short acting insulin before meals and an intermediate acting insulin before bed with a snack.

ENDOCRINOLOGY: MULTIPLE CHOICE ANSWERS

1.26   B C E

Although craniopharyngiomas arise from embryonic remnants (Rathke's pouch), they not infrequently present for the first time in adulthood. Unlike true pituitary tumours, they arise above the pituitary fossa and therefore can damage the hypothalamus (and ADH secreting neurones) without compressing the pituitary causing diabetes insipidus, and disturbances of sleep, appetite and temperature regulation. Downward expansion may cause chiasmatic or optic nerve compression. The tumour is typically cystic, calcified in 35% of adult cases and although never malignant, is almost impossible to excise completely, responds poorly to radiotherapy and may require repeated cyst drainage.

1.27   C

IGF-1 (previously known as somatomedin C) is produced predominantly in the liver in response to circulating growth hormone (GH) and mediates the majority of the growth promoting actions of GH. Unlike GH, it has a long plasma half-life and hence a random raised serum level is a useful diagnostic indicator of acromegaly. Levels fall rapidly during illness and starvation. IGF circulates at concentrations 1000 times higher than that of insulin and can cross react with the insulin receptor but binding to six different IGF binding proteins (to which insulin does not bind) prevents this *in vivo*. Within tissues, enzymes are secreted which cleave the binding proteins releasing the IGF-1 to act as a growth factor locally.

1.28   C D E

Glucose, as in the glucose tolerance test, suppresses GH levels. Failure to suppress in this test is used to diagnose acromegaly. Somatostatin and dopamine agonists also suppress GH secretion and are used therapeutically in acromegaly. GH secretion is pulsatile with increased frequency and amplitude of 'spikes' during sleep, exercise and stress. Additional stimulators of GH release include hypoglycaemia (as in insulin tolerance test), glucagon, amino acids such as arginine and lysine (as in Bovril), hypothalamic GH-releasing hormone (GHRH) and a newly identified range of synthetic hexapeptides (hexarelin, GH releasing peptides or GHRPs) derived from the structure of metenkephalin, all of which have been used in tests for GH deficiency.

1.29   A B C

Isolated deficiencies of gonadotrophins or growth hormone are well described and may be due to failure of secretion of their respective hypothalamic releasing hormones. Concomitant cortisol deficiency reduces the severity of and may even conceal diabetes insipidus, possibly because it lowers glomerular filtration rate. DI may therefore be revealed by adrenal replacement therapy. In combined adrenal and thyroid failure, an adrenal crisis may be precipitated by starting thyroxine replacement therapy before corticosteroids. Aldosterone synthesis and secretion occur in the zona glomerulosa of the adrenal cortex and are largely ACTH-independent. Mineralocorticoid deficiency sufficient to require replacement therapy is therefore rare in hypopituitarism. Fertility depends on the gonadotrophins, which must be replaced for fertility to be achieved.

1.30   D E

Growth hormone secreting (somatotroph) pituitary tumours are almost always macroadenomas (>1cm) and frequently expand beyond the sella. Random GH levels are of no use in diagnosing acromegaly as levels taken during a 'spike' will be raised in normal people (see Q37). Somatotroph tumours often co-secrete or immunostain for prolactin as well as GH and over 80% co-secrete the alpha subunit of the glycoprotein hormones. Associated features of acromegaly include sleep apnoea, multiple skin tags, adenomatous polyps and hypercalcuria causing renal stones due to a direct renal tubular action of GH. The presence of hypercalcaemia suggests hyperparathyroidism associated with multiple endocrine neoplasia (MEN) 1 syndrome.

1.31   B D

ADH is a nonapeptide synthesised in neurones in the hypothalamus (mostly the supraoptic and paraventricular nuclei). It is transported (bound to neurophysin carrier proteins) along axons descending the pituitary stalk to the posterior pituitary, where it is released into the circulation. Its release is stimulated by high plasma osmolality, hypovolaemia, smoking and by many drugs including morphine, chlorpropamide and carbamazepine (the last two are used to treat partial cranial diabetes insipidus). ADH secretion is suppressed by naloxone, phenytoin and ethanol.

1.32   A B E

Deficiency of antidiuretic hormone (central DI) or impaired action on the kidney collecting ducts (nephrogenic DI) causes polydypsia and polyuria resulting in dehydration. With a normal thirst mechanism, treatment is not essential. Urinary fluid losses can be compensated for by drinking more although the serum remains slightly concentrated (raised sodium concentration, typically >140 mmol/l). The nephrogenic form may be caused by drugs such as lithium, hypercalcaemia, hypokalaemia, intrinsic renal disease (e.g. polycystic kidneys) or be inherited as an X-linked trait.

1.33   B E

Galactorrhoea is invariably due to hyperprolactinaemia or an increased sensitivity of the breast to prolactin. Prolactin secretion is under dominant negative control by dopamine from the hypothalamus and hence hypothalamic damage or dopamine antagonists such as the major tranquillisers and anti-emetics (e.g. metoclopramide) cause hyperprolactinaemia. Anti-depressants have little anti-dopaminergic action and rarely cause significant increases in prolactin. Hyperprolactinaemia and galactorrhoea occur independently of gynaecomastia which is due to raised oestrogen levels (e.g. from drugs, tumours or liver disease). Prolactin microadenomas (<1 cm) are the commonest cause of galactorrhoea in women. Prolactin levels are also raised in pregnancy, by stress and by raised TRH levels in primary hypothyroidism.

1.34   B

Anorexia nervosa is associated with a number of endocrine abnormalities, most apparently due to malnutrition or weight loss. These include low gonadotrophin levels with loss of the normal pulsatile pattern of secretion (a profile typical of prepubertal girls), high-normal or supranormal cortisol levels (possibly related to depression), and high growth hormone levels (possibly due to reduced negative feedback on the pituitary by low circulating levels of insulin-like growth factors). The eating disorder and weight loss may begin before menarche and so prevent pubertal gonadotrophin release and the appearance of puberty itself. An elevated ESR suggests organic disease (the ESR is normal or low in anorexia), whereas loss of pubic hair suggests hypopituitarism (in anorexia, pubic hair is conserved and fine, dark lanugo hair may appear on the body and face).

1.35   A B C E

Circulating testosterone is mainly bound to sex-hormone binding globulin, the levels of which are generally inversely related to prevailing testosterone concentrations. Hypogonadotrophic hypogonadism may be associated with impaired or absent sense of smell (Kallmann's syndrome). In the testicular feminisation syndrome the gonads are undescended testes (intra-abdominal or in the inguinal canal) and are therefore at increased risk of malignancy. Typical 47,XXY individuals with Klinefelter's syndrome often show complete seminiferous tubule dysgenesis and therefore azoospermia, but others (especially mosaics) may be relatively well masculinised and rare cases have produced spermatozoa. Klinefelter's syndrome is the commonest cause of bilateral testicular failure resulting in hypogonadism with raised FSH/LH (hypergonadotrophic). It is not inherited but caused by chromosomal non-dysjunction in the sperm/ova or, rarely, post-fertilisation (3% of cases).

1.36   E

In Graves' disease, thyroid stimulation is due to activation of the TSH receptors by autoantibodies which develop against the receptor. By contrast, autoantibodies directed against other thyroid components (e.g. microsomes of the follicular cells or thyroglobulin) cause damage rather than stimulation of the gland. Elevated thyroxine and tri-iodothyronine levels act through negative feedback on the hypothalamus and pituitary to reduce secretion of TSH, the circulating levels of which are suppressed to below the normal range. Thyroid eye disease is often temporally separated from the hyperthyroidism. Amenorrhoea is a recognised feature of thyrotoxicosis of any cause. Neonatal hyperthyroidism results from IgG TSH-receptor-stimulating antibodies which cross the placenta and stimulate the fetal thyroid; it resolves spontaneously after some weeks when the antibodies are cleared from the circulation. Only a small amount of maternal thyroxine crosses the placenta.

1.37   A C D E

Autoimmune thyroid failure is associated with other organ-specific autoimmune disease; the combination with Addison's disease is referred to as 'Schmidt's syndrome'. Pericardial and pleural effusions and ascites, reversible with thyroid replacement, may occur. Rare neurological complications include bilateral cerebellar damage and 'myxoedema madness' (first described by Richard Asher), which includes hallucinations, agitation, delusions and paranoia. Localised 'myxoedema' consisting of cutaneous hyaluronic acid deposits and most often appearing on the shins, is a feature of Graves' disease.

1.38   A B D E

Self-limiting thyrotoxicosis due to discharge of stored hormone (often followed by transient hypothyroidism) is seen in de Quervain's post-viral thyroiditis associated with a raised ESR. Iodine uptake into the thyroid is low and new thyroid hormone synthesis is suppressed. A similar pattern of self-limiting thyroid disturbance may be seen in the postpartum period, so-called postpartum thyroiditis, believed to be of autoimmune origin. Treatment in either case is symptomatic with beta blockers. Carbimazole is ineffective. In thyrotoxicosis of any cause, surgery is reserved for refractory or non-compliant cases. Diarrhoea, proximal muscle weakness, leucopenia and rarely periodic muscle paralysis (especially in Chinese) are manifestations of thyrotoxicosis.

1.39   A B C D

Over 99% of circulating T4 is bound to plasma proteins, mainly thyroid-binding globulin (TBG) but also pre-albumin and albumin. Oestrogen raises TBG levels (e.g. pregnancy, oral contraceptive) and hence total thyroxine concentrations. Congenitally low or high TBG levels may occur and nephrotic syndrome may lower TBG along with other serum proteins. High hCG levels in early pregnancy and especially hyperemesis gravidarum cross-react with the TSH receptor causing mild hyperthyroidism with low TSH. The high iodine content of amiodarone may cause hyper- or hypothyroidism. Treatment with cytokines such as interferons or interleukin-2 may precipitate or exacerbate autoimmune hypothyroidism. In acute illness, the syndrome of 'sick euthyroidism' is seen with rapid falls in free T3 followed by reduced levels of TSH and free T4.

1.40   A C E

Membrane G proteins mediate signalling via cyclic AMP by linking surface membrane receptors for certain glycoprotein hormones (e.g. GHRH, TSH, ACTH, glucagon, catecholamines) to the adenylate cyclase enzyme that generates cyclic AMP. They are so-called because they hydrolyse GTP on activation. Inhibitory G proteins (Gi) mediate suppression of adenylate cyclase by somatostatin. G protein mutations that cause constitutive adenylate cyclase activation have been found in growth hormone pituitary tumours, thyroid tumours and precocious puberty associated with McCune Albright syndrome. Mutations that prevent cyclic AMP generation impair parathyroid hormone action in pseudohypoparathyroidism.

1.41   A B C E

Features of cortisol excess in Cushing's syndrome due to all causes include central fat deposition (including the round 'moon', face, 'buffalo' hump and supraclavicular fat pads), subconjunctival oedema (a useful physical sign) and growth retardation or arrest in children. Functional adrenal tumours (both benign adenoma and carcinoma) often produce excess androgen and/or oestrogen in addition to cortisol; marked masculinisation (including clitoromegaly) or feminisation therefore suggests an adrenal tumour rather than pituitary-driven Cushing's disease, in which excess sex steroid production is rare. Primary adrenal over-production of cortisol suppresses ACTH secretion; very high ACTH levels and pronounced hyperpigmentation suggest that Cushing's syndrome is driven by an 'ectopic' source of ACTH such as a lung or pancreatic carcinoid.

1.42   B

ANP is a 28 amino-acid peptide synthesised by the myocytes of the right atrium and ventricle and released in response to volume overload as detected by increased right atrial stretch. It corrects the hypervolaemia by effects which oppose those of angiotensin and aldosterone: increasing renal sodium excretion, vasodilatation, reducing thirst and salt craving as well as inhibiting the actions of renin, aldosterone and ADH. Its true physiological importance remains unclear.

1.43   B C

Individual requirements for glucocorticoid replacement vary widely: some patients require as little as 5 mg/day whereas others may need 30 mg/day. Symptoms suggestive of inadequate replacement include tiredness, loss of energy, anorexia, vomiting, headache and 'flu-like' malaise; postural hypotension, hyperkalaemia and an elevated blood urea concentration may also be present. Insomnia may be due to overreplacement or to taking the evening dose too late. Other features of overdosage include excessive weight gain (especially if with oedema or Cushingoid features), hypertension and hypokalaemia.

1.44   A B C D E

CAH is a group of diseases due to inherited deficiencies of various steroid biosynthetic enzymes, of which 21-hydroxylase is the most commonly affected. The manifestations of CAH depend on the site of the enzyme defect and on the relative effects of 'upstream' precursor excesses and of end-product deficiency. Cortisol deficiency may be severe and fatal in the neonatal period. With 21-hydroxylase defects, 17-hydroxyprogesterone and androgenic steroids accumulate, causing virilisation. Glucocorticoid treatment not only replaces cortisol but also suppresses androgenic precursors, and can prevent virilism; 17-hydroxyprogesterone and testosterone levels are useful guides to adjusting dosage. Life-threatening hypoglycaemia may accompany cortisol deficiency due to intercurrent illness or omission of steroids.

1.45   A B E

Hypoparathyroidism may be due to autoimmune disease, when autoantibodies are often directed against several tissues and may produce clinical disease including hypothyroidism, Addison's disease, type 1 diabetes, primary ovarian failure and pernicious anaemia. Chronic mucocutaneous candidiasis is common in hypoparathyroidism associated with autoimmune disease and in Di George syndrome. Calcification of the basal ganglia occurs in both hypoparathyroidism and pseudohypoparathyroidism (which is due to target organ resistance to parathyroid hormone, not to parathyroid failure), but is rarely associated with Parkinsonism. Several somatic features (including short stature, 'moon-face' and short metacarpals and metatarsals) occur in pseudohypoparathyroidism, but not in true hypoparathyroidism. Both hypoparathyroidism and pseudohypoparathyroidism are treated with calcium supplements and vitamin D derivatives such as alfacalcidol; parathyroid hormone is not currently available for practical therapeutic use.

1.46   C D

Paget's disease is believed to be primarily an osteoclast disorder, although coupled increases in osteoblast activity are required for new bone formation. Disease activity is indicated by urinary hydroxyproline or pyridinium–collagen crosslinks but serum alkaline phosphatase is often the simplest indicator. Complications include pain, bone/skull deformity, deafness, paraplegia, high-output cardiac failure, pathological fracture and osteosarcoma. Radiological evidence of extensive disease alone is insufficient indication for treatment. Effective treatments are calcitonin, mithramycin and bisphosphonates, the last being currently the most common choice.

1.47   A C E

The MEN 1 syndrome comprises two or more of the following: parathyroid tumours (hyperplasia is commoner than adenoma, and carcinoma is very rare), pituitary tumours, and pancreatic endocrine tumours. The latter include insulinoma, glucagonoma, gastrinoma, carcinoid, VIPoma (causing the Verner–Morrison syndrome of watery diarrhoea, hypokalaemia and achlorhydria) and rare tumours producing growth hormone releasing hormone, which can cause acromegaly. Medullary carcinoma of the thyroid, phaeochromocytoma and parathyroid tumours define the MEN-2 syndrome; multiple facial neuromata (especially of the eyelids, tongue and lips) occur in a variant of MEN-2 syndrome, previously classified as 2B and now described separately as MEN-3. MEN-2A has been linked to the *ret* proto-oncogene in chromosome 10.

1.48   B C

In both normal and neoplastic β-cells, proinsulin is cleaved enzymatically to produce equimolar amounts of insulin and C-peptide. Hypoglycaemia caused by exogenous insulin (which contains virtually no C-peptide) inhibits pancreatic insulin release and circulating C-peptide levels are therefore low. In insulinomas, defective post- translational processing of proinsulin may allow proinsulin to be secreted in addition to insulin and C-peptide. Virtually all patients with an insulinoma will become hypoglycaemic (venous plasma glucose concentration 3.5 mmol/l) and neuroglycopenic during a 72-hour fast. The tolbutamide test is dangerous and now obsolete. Nesidio-blastosis is diffuse β-cell hyperplasia occurring throughout the pancreas, in contrast to the focal β-cell proliferation of insulinomas. Although rare, it is a common cause of hyperinsulinaemia and hypo-glycaemia in early childhood, when discrete insulinomas are rare.

1.49   B E

Ten per cent of phaeochromocytomas lie outside the adrenal medulla, and even those in the classical site may not be detected by CT scan. The presence of large tumours may be deduced from displacement of the renal outline on an IVP. In addition to adrenaline (which predominates in adrenal phaeochromocytomas) and noradrenaline (extra- adrenal tumours), dopamine may be secreted, especially by malignant tumours. Phaeochromocytomas occur in association with medullary carcinoma of the thyroid and parathyroid tumours (MEN-2), but not with pancreatic endocrine or pituitary tumours (MEN-1). Treatment with β-blockers alone is hazardous: removal of β-adrenergic vasodilation in skeletal muscle may cause a hypertensive crisis. Treatment should therefore start with an α-blocker (e.g. phenoxybenzamine), to which a β-blocker may be added to control tachycardia.

1.50   B D E

Calcitonin-gene related peptide is a peptide encoded within the calcitonin gene complex, but with entirely different actions. It has no effect on calcium metabolism but is a powerful vasodilator. Secretory diarrhoea occurs in most patients with gastrinoma and is mainly due to acid hypersecretion. DDAVP is an analogue of arginine vasopressin which, unlike the native peptide has virtually no vasoconstrictor activity and can therefore be used in patients with ischaemic heart disease. Gastrin release is inhibited by the presence of acid in the stomach; reduced acid secretion (as in the atrophic gastritis of pernicious anaemia) therefore stimulates gastrin secretion.

GASTROENTEROLOGY: 'BEST OF FIVE'
ANSWERS

2.1 E: Primary sclerosing cholangitis

This cholestatic picture is due to primary sclerosing cholangitis (PSC). PSC in UC is associated with ANCA in 80% of patients. It is more common in men than in women. Primary biliary cirrhosis is very uncommon in men. Alcoholic hepatitis gives a hepatitic picture, not one of cholestasis. Azathioprine can cause abnormal LFTs, but this usually settles within the first month. Liver metastases are a possibility, but less likely than PSC.

2.2 C: Bacterial overgrowth secondary to an enterocolic fistula

This is a picture of malabsorption for which the main differential diagnoses are active small bowel Crohn's disease and a fistula, with bacterial overgrowth. The laboratory tests do not indicate an inflammatory process. Acquired lactose intolerance can give bloating and diarrhoea, but not anaemia or low albumin. Bile salt diarrhoea is watery, but not associated with colic or systemic symptoms. Strictures are associated with colic, but will not cause anaemia and a low albumin unless there is bacteria overgrowth too. So, only a fistula with overgrowth will fully explain the symptoms.

2.3 A: Coeliac disease

This is a picture of malabsorption. 'Silent' malabsorption of this type strongly suggests coeliac disease. The mouth ulcers are associated with coeliac disease or Crohn's disease, however there are no other symptoms to suggest Crohn's disease. In general, giardiasis and Crohn's disease are associated with gastrointestinal symptoms in addition to malabsorption. Scleroderma has characteristic extra-intestinal signs.

2.4 D: Refer for endoscopy

Gastric ulcers, particularly in patients with 'alarm symptoms', should be biopsied. Weight loss and anaemia are alarm symptoms. Benign ulcers rarely if ever present with anaemia. If this patient is found to have a benign ulcer, then his colon should be investigated.

2.5 A: Barium enema

Occult blood loss in a man of this age is due to a caecal cancer until proved otherwise. This is the age at which the incidence of such cancers rises significantly. FOB testing is pointless, in the absence of overt blood loss, a non-vegetarian either has malabsorption or GI bleeding; a negative FOB would not rule out bleeding. A red cell scan is only useful during an episode of bleeding. Upper GI malignancy is less common, but should be sought if the barium enema is normal.

2.6   C: Reassure her with explanation of the diagnosis, without further investigation

Her symptoms are those of irritable bowel syndrome. In most patients the cause is stress. Investigations are not called for in patients of this age, if at any age. Reassurance with a careful explanation of the problem is all that is usually required.

2.7   D: Migration of the PEG with pyloric obstruction

This is a picture of upper GI obstruction. PEG migration is the most likely diagnosis.

2.8   D: High dose PPI, reducing later

NICE guidelines support the stance of most gastroenterologists – to use an effective proton pump inhibitor (PPI), the dose of which is reduced once symptoms come under control. In patients of this age, who are unlikely to be taking other drugs and so are not at risk of drug interactions, price is the main determinant of the choice of PPI. A cost-effectiveness study has shown the antireflux surgery is not useful in most patients as they relapse later and then take PPI therapy once more.

2.9   D: Paracentesis/albumin/glypressin

This is type 1 hepatorenal failure. It occurs in patients with cirrhosis complicated by ascites and mild stable renal impairment (type 2 hepatorenal syndrome) who then have reduced renal perfusion due to sepsis or blood loss. The untreated mortality is 90% at 2 weeks, but the paracentesis/albumin/glypressin regimen lowers mortality and corrects renal failure in most patients.

2.10   B: Hepatitis A

The picture is one of fulminant hepatic failure (FHF). Paracetamol and hepatitis A are the most likely causes, however the duration of the antecedent history and the absence of a history of paracetamol overdose, makes hepatitis A the most likely diagnosis. All patients in this condition should be referred to a Liver Unit. Hepatitis A serology may be negative at presentation.

2.11   D: Primary biliary cirrhosis

Primary biliary cirrhosis (PBC) is the most likely diagnosis. Itching is often the first symptom. PBC is most common in middle-aged women. The LFTs typically show a cholestatic pattern. Antimitochrondrial antibodies are expected.

2.12   B: Acute pancreatitis

This is acute pancreatitis. However, all the others are reasonable differential diagnoses. Opiate withdrawal is not usually accompanied by shock, nor are cholecystitis and alcoholic hepatitis. Fever is present in alcoholic hepatitis, cholecystitis and sometimes in a perforated DU, however in none of these does the pain usually radiate to the back.

2.13   C: Oesophageal variceal endoscopic ligation

Ligation is the treatment of choice, if an appropriately skilled endoscopist is available. Sclerotherapy is probably the next best choice although glypressin is very useful. TIPSS should be reserved as a salvage technique when other approaches have failed.

2.14   A: Azathioprine

Azathioprine is the only option to consider at this stage. Long term steroids are not indicated in Crohn's disease. Cyclosporin does not work. Infliximab is only licensed for active disease that is refractory to steroids and first line immunosuppressives. Methotrexate causes miscarriage.

2.15   E: Gilbert's syndrome

The most likely diagnosis is Gilbert's syndrome. The only biochemical abnormality of the bilirubin. The other diagnoses each have an elevated transaminase when the bilirubin is raised. Gilbert's syndrome is common, although the jaundice is usually only clinically apparent during an intercurrent illness.

2.16   D: PPI treatment with repeat endoscopy in 3–6 months

There is a significant risk of Barrett's oesophagus and adenocarcinoma arising in such a patient. Peptic strictures may also occur. Severe oesophagitis may lead to dysphagia even without a stricture. Severe dysplasia should be confirmed by repeat endoscopy in the presence of acid blockade. If confirmed, oesophagectomy should be performed.

2.17   E: Solitary rectal ulcer

The site of the lesion is characteristic. Solitary rectal ulcers are associated with straining at stool and trauma (due to digitally assisted evacuation for example). The lesion may resemble a tumour, so a biopsy is essential.

2.18   C: Pneumatosis coli

The gas-filled blebs are characteristic. Pneumatosis coli is associated with COPD and usually presents with rectal bleeding and diarrhoea. Antibiotic diarrhoea may be accompanied by blood and is a reasonable thought in a patient likely to have been exposed to antibiotics, but duration of the symptoms is too long. The patient is too old to have familial adenomatous polyposis.

2.19   A: CMV proctitis

CMV proctitis is painless, unlike herpes proctitis. Inclusion bodies are characteristic.

2.20   D: Portal vein thrombosis

Bleeding oesophageal varices in the absence of signs of chronic liver disease strongly suggest portal vein thrombosis. SCBU treatment is likely to be associated with umbilical vein cannulation with the attendant risk of sepsis and portal vein thrombosis.

2.21   B: Hydatid disease

Hydatid disease is usually asymptomatic. The infestation is acquired by exposure to faeces containing *Echinococcus* eggs. The internal acoustic shadows are the key to the ultrasonographic diagnosis.

2.22   E: Metformin

Metformin is a common cause of diarrhoea. However, all the others are plausible.

2.23   E: Peristomal abscess

Peristomal inflammation will lead to diarrhoea. The investigations are consistent with an abscess. Bile salt diarrhoea only occurs if the colon is in continuity.

2.24   C: Heller's myotomy

The diagnosis is achalasia. Heller's myotomy is the treatment of choice in a young patient. Botulinum toxin is useful for short-term relief of symptoms for patients who are not fit for surgery.

2.25   A: Boerhaave's syndrome

This is a characteristic presentation of this life-threatening disorder. The oesophagus is ruptured during severe vomiting. Perforation usually occurs to the left, giving rise to mediastinal and pericardial emphysema and a left pleural effusion.

GASTROENTEROLOGY: MULTIPLE CHOICE ANSWERS

2.26   D

Acid secretion in response to a meal has three phases, cephalic, gastric and duodenal. The main stimulus for acid secretion is neuronal, predominantly vagal cholinergic neurons. Gastrin is released from antral G cells and acts indirectly on the parietal cell via histamine released from ECL cells. In addition to stimulating release of histamine from ECL cells, gastrin also has a trophic action on these cells. Gastrin is also found in neurons of the central nervous system, although its function is unknown.

2.27   A B D E

Over 95% of patients with primary biliary cirrhosis have positive serum antimitochondrial antibodies, although they are not specific for primary biliary cirrhosis since positive results occur in some other liver diseases. Excess liver accumulation of copper accompanies the cholestasis, but is not usually sufficient to cause confusion with Wilson's disease. Centri-zonal necrosis is not a feature. Associated conditions include rheumatoid arthritis, scleroderma, Sjögren's syndrome, pancreatic atrophy and renal tubular acidosis.

2.28   E

Acute massive hepatocellular necrosis following paracetamol usually produces acidosis early on. Early referral for transplant assessment should be considered when pH falls below 7.31 and either the prothrombin time is >100 seconds or the plasma creatinine is >300 mmol/l. Serum albumin has a plasma half life of 14–16 days and is no indication of hepatocellular damage in the acute setting. Similarly bilirubin takes days to accumulate and jaundice is a late feature, often not appearing until fulminant hepatic failure is obvious. Intravenous N-acetyl cysteine is the treatment of choice and should be commenced as soon as possible after presentation.

2.29   A C

Chronic atrophic gastritis is an autoimmune inflammation centred on the parietal cell, often present for years before pernicious anaemia develops. The standard diagnostic test remains the Shilling test. The resulting achlorhydria leads to hypergastrinaemia, which in some patients induces mucosal endocrine cell hyperplasia, benign endocrine cell polyps and rarely, gastric carcinoid tumours. Endoscopic surveillance is of unproven benefit, but a single endoscopy at diagnosis may be of value in detection of early adenocarcinoma, present in approximately 5% of patients at diagnosis.

2.30   A B C

Whilst cirrhosis and portal hypertension are the commonest causes of variceal haemorrhage, any cause of portal hypertension will result in varices e.g. portal vein thrombosis or compression. Prognosis depends on the severity of the underlying liver disease. Endoscopy to confirm the diagnosis and attempt to prevent further blood loss by oesophageal banding or sclerotherapy should be performed after resuscitation. Intravenous octreotide is effective treatment in arresting haemorrhage and is as effective as sclerotherapy in continuous bleeding.

2.31   A

Epidemiological studies have shown that a diet high in animal fat and low in fruit and vegetable fibre predisposes to colon cancer. Familial adenomatous polyposis coli (FAPC) is an uncommon disorder, inherited in autosomal dominant manner and inevitably results in colon cancer. It accounts for approximately 1% of all cases. The FAPC gene is located on chromosome 5. In contrast, hereditary non-polyposiscolorrectal cancer (HNPCC) is relatively common accounting for up to 15% of cases of colon cancer. The familial colorectal cancer gene is linked to chromosome 2 and is also dominantly inherited. Faecal occult blood testing is a sensitive test for gastointestinal blood loss but its sensitivity and specifity is too low for it to be of value in the detection of colon cancer.

2.32   A C E

Intestinal infection in the acquired immunodeficiency syndrome is common. In the oesophagus, herpes simplex, *Candida albicans* or cytomegalovirus may be the causative agent. Opportunistic small bowel disease occurs with cryptosporidium, *Isospora belli*, other sporing protozoa or atypical mycobacteria such as *Myobacterium avium* and *M. intracellulare* mimicking Whipple's disease. Colitis may be due to herpes simplex or cytomegalovirus. Gastrointestinal Kaposi's sarcoma may be the initial presentation of AIDS. *Cryptococcus neoformans* usually causes a meningitis and *Pneumocystis* a pneumonia.

2.33   C E

H. pylori is a Gram-negative *Campylobacter*-like organism that survives in the mucous layer of the gastric mucosa close to the epithelium. Its prevalence increases with age and the presence of the organism can be diagnosed by the urease breath test, the bacteria producing urease which breaks down ingested C13-labelled urea to ammonia and carbon dioxide which can be detected in exhaled air. The presence of *H. pylori* carries a 6-fold increased risk for the development of gastric carcinoma.

2.34   C E

Coeliac disease is associated with HLA B8 and DR3. Dietary exposure to gluten results in intestinal inflammation most severe in the jejunum. Histologically there is a lymphocytic infiltrate in the lamina propria together with increased intraepithelial lymphocytes. Whilst villus height is lost, crypt length is increased reflecting increased cell turnover. Coeliac disease is associated with a number of neurological syndromes including epilepsy, and reversible infertility has been described in both men and women.

2.35   B C

Pseudomembranous colitis describes the development of colonic inflammation in association with the use of antimicrobial drugs. Clindamycin was the antibiotic initially associated with this condition, but many broad spectrum antibiotics are now implicated. The cause is infection with a toxin-producing strain of *Clostridium difficile*. Multiple raised yellowish-white plaques are seen predominantly in the distal colon, although on rare occasions the rectum is spared. *C. difficile*, but not the toxin, may be found in the stools of 3% of normal adults and up to 50% of healthy neonates. Treatment is with oral vancomycin, oral or intravenous metronidazole or oral bacitracin. Relapse occurs in up to 33% of cases.

2.36   A C D

Pain is a prominent clinical feature in the majority of patients early on, but pain may lessen as the disease progresses and may disappear completely with end stage disease. Less commonly, patients may present with malabsorption without pain. Portal hypertension may be a result of peripancreatic fibrosis and compression of the portal vein. Although overt jaundice is relatively unknown, biliary strictures occur in >30% of patients with chronic pancreatitis.

2.37   A C

Folic acid is found in liver, nuts and green vegetables but is degraded by cooking. Absorption of the daily requirement of 100–200 µg occurs in the duodenum and jejunum. Body stores are sufficient for 4 months. Causes of folate malabsorption include coeliac disease, tropical sprue, jejunal and gastric resection, intestinal lymphoma, and drugs particularly methotrexate and sulphasalazine. In stagnant loop syndrome, folic acid is synthesised by bacteria and blood concentrations are increased. Alcoholic macrocytosis does not respond to folate supplementation.

2.38   A D

Constructional apraxia, inversion of normal sleep pattern, flapping tremor, hepatic foetor and personality disturbances are all well recognised clinical features of hepatic encephalopathy. In addition, brisk tendon reflexes, increased muscle tone and rigidity are common clinical findings. Pupillary responses are preserved.

2.39   B E

The solitary rectal ulcer syndrome is most common in women in their third decade. It is associated with constipation and disordered defaecation due to perineal descent and anterior rectal prolapse. Trauma and or ischaemia of the anterior rectal wall leads to ulceration, with approximately 80% of all ulcers being sited here. Perineal pain, soiling, mucous discharge and rectal bleeding are common symptoms, the latter leading to iron deficiency anaemia in some cases.

2.40   B C D

The main physiological actions of cholecystokinin are to stimulate gall bladder contraction and pancreatic exocrine secretion. Its direct effect on smooth muscle is to cause contraction but it acts via a vagal reflex to produce fundal relaxation and hence delayed gastric emptying. Cholecystokinin has been extensively studied as a potential mediator of satiety.

2.41   B C D

Although the irritable bowel syndrome (IBS) is believed to represent disordered intestinal smooth muscle function, no characteristic abnormality of intestinal motility has been demonstrated. A lowered threshold to intraluminal distension is a common finding and reflects a heightened sensitivity. Other organs may also be involved, dysmenorrhoea, dysuria and urinary frequency being common associations. IBS can be precipitated by travellers' diarrhoea only in those subjects with a pre-existing affective disorder.

2.42   A E

Wilson's disease is a rare inherited disorder of copper metabolism characterised by failure of biliary excretion of copper. There is an accumulation of copper within the liver, decreased serum caeruloplasmin and accumulation of copper in the brain, predominantly the basal ganglia. Neurological manifestations include isolated psychiatric illness and more commonly a Parkinsonian movement disorder. Copper deposits also appear in Descemet's membrane close to the limbus of the cornea – Kayser-Fleischer rings.

2.43   B D E

Bilirubin is formed from haem, but only 70% from haemoglobin, the remainder coming from non-erythroid haem and haemoproteins often in the liver. Unconjugated bilirubin, which makes up virtually all the serum bilirubin in normal subjects, is water insoluble, and therefore is transported to the liver bound to serum albumin. In the liver it is conjugated with glucuronic acid to increase water solubility and facilitate excretion. In the gut it is metabolised by gut bacteria to urobilinogen which undergoes an enterohepatic circulation.

2.44   C

The *c-ret* oncogene codes for a tyrosine kinase which is normally expressed in the embryo in developing neuroendocrine cells of the gastrointestinal tract and elsewhere. Mutation may therefore lead to failure of normal developmental migration of intestinal neurons leading to Hirschsprung's disease, or predisposition to neuroendocrine tumours. Hence mutations of the *c-ret* oncogene also account for the MEN syndromes 2 A and B. The gene for MEN 1, which includes Zollinger-Ellison syndrome and the gene for haemochromatosis have not yet been cloned and that for cystic fibrosis codes for the cystic fibrosis transmembrane conductance regulator.

2.45   D

Patients with gastro-oesophageal reflux disease (GORD) usually reflux acid into their distal oesophagus. The resulting acid-induced damage produces mucosal inflammation and also may reduce oesophageal clearance which improves with successful treatment. Oesophageal clearance may however be of primary aetiological significance as in systemic sclerosis, where poor clearance prolongs exposure to acid. Odynophagia is a characteristic symptom of GORD, which is most accurately diagnosed by 24 hour pH monitoring. For acid reflux, proton pump inhibitors with or without a prokinetic provide the best symptomatic relief.

2.46   A B D E

The gastrointestinal tract is frequently affected in systemic sclerosis with the oesophagus being involved in up to 80% of patients. Abnormalities are best seen by manometry and include low resting oesophageal pressure and non-progressive contractions. Symptoms include heartburn, dysphagia for liquids and solids and pulmonary aspiration on lying down. Stomach involvement is rare, but systemic sclerosis causes dilatation and stasis of the small intestine and delayed transit. Abdominal pain, distension, diarrhoea and steatorrhoea, which is probably due to bacterial overgrowth, may occur. Colonic symptoms are uncommon. Systemic sclerosis is associated with autoimmune disease such as primary biliary cirrhosis and the CREST syndrome.

2.47   C D

Ingested fat is predominantly triglyceride and is broken down by pancreatic lipase to free fatty acids or monoglyceride. Fatty acid stimulates cholecystokinin release from mucosal endocrine cells of the small intestine resulting in gallbladder contraction and delivery of bile salts to the intestine. Bile salts aid micelle formation by emulsification with fatty acids and monoglyceride which are then absorbed. Any unabsorbed fat reaching the distal small intestine slows intestinal transit, a reflex termed the ileal brake.

2.48   A E

The use of mesalazine to maintain remission in ulcerative colitis is well established. More recently high doses of slow-release mesalazine have been shown to be effective in the treatment of active small bowel Crohn's disease. Generally 5-acetylsalicylic acid compounds are safe in pregnancy and do not produce impotence, although sulphasalazine causes oligospermia, a side effect attributable to its sulphapyridine moiety. Acetylsalicylic acid foam enemas are now available as effective treatment for colitis of the rectosigmoid colon.

2.49   A C D

The delayed gastric emptying seen in diabetic patients with gastroparesis can be effectively treated by the motilin receptor agonist erythromycin. Gastroparesis may affect diabetic control and hyperglycaemia contributes to the delayed gastric emptying by reducing vagal tone to the stomach. Anti-Parkinsonian drugs by merit of their anti-cholinergic and or dopaminergic effects also slow gastric emptying. No consistent gastric motility disorder has been identified in functional dyspepsia although 50% of patients may show delayed gastric emptying.

2.50   A C E

C. difficile can be found as part of the normal colonic flora in about 3% of healthy adults. Its toxin is detectable in nearly all patients with pseudomembranous colitis and in up to 33% of those with less severe antibiotic related diarrhoea. Presentation varies from self-limiting diarrhoea to fulminating colitis with toxic dilatation. First line therapy should be oral metronidazole and if this fails oral vancomycin, but both may be given intravenously if necessary.

NEPHROLOGY: 'BEST OF FIVE' ANSWERS

3.1   E: It is often associated with eosinophilia

Cholesterol emboli to the kidneys usually arise from an atheromatous aorta, and may be triggered by instrumentation (e.g. arteriography). They are found at autopsy in 17% of patients over 60 years of age, although they may be subclinical. The crystals usually lodge in arteries of diameter 150–300 mm, so complete renal infarction resulting in loin pain and haematuria is rare. There is typically evidence of microinfarcts elsewhere on the lower extremities, such as livedo reticularis and gangrenous toes. Leucocytosis, eosinophilia and reduced C3 are typical but not invariable findings.

3.2   B: Pulsed methylprednisolone may be used in treatment

Hepatitis C causes an immune complex mediated membranoproliferative glomerulonephritis. The immunoglobulins are not cold agglutinins (antibodies causing agglutination of erythrocytes in the cold peripheries of the body), but cryoglobulins (types II and III mixed). Cryoglobulins are immunoglobulins that reversibly precipitate in the cold. One-third of patients exhibit spontaneous renal remission. Alpha interferon is used in treatment; pulsed methylprednisolone and plasma exchange are also of value.

3.3   E: Mesangial widening, basement membrane thickening and capillary obliteration

Hyaline thrombi are found in monoclonal immunoglobulin deposition diseases, SLE and thrombotic microangiopathies. The typical changes of membranous glomerulonephritis include capillary thickening, and spike and chain appearance of the basement membrane. Mesangial hypercellularity is seen in the proliferative glomerulopathies: post streptococcal, mesangiocapillary, IgA/HSP, SLE, vasculitides, endocarditis. Green birefringence on staining with Congo Red is a feature of amyloidosis.

3.4   E: Normal PTH levels

The 1, 25 dihydroxycholecalciferol is low or normal, not (as would be expected for the degree of hypophosphataemia) elevated. There is renal phosphate wasting, but glycosuria and aminoaciduria are absent. The condition is X-linked but females may be affected by lyonization.

3.5 B: Gastric ulceration is partly attributable to increased rate of *Helicobacter pylori* carriage

Cardiovascular death is the most important cause of death following transplantation. The risk of malignancy is much increased after transplantation; in rarer tumours the risk may be increased by a factor of 1000.

Another predisposing risk factor for gastric ulceration is prednisolone therapy.

With regard to infective complications, reverse barrier nursing is now considered unnecessary. A CMV-negative recipient should not receive a kidney from a CMV-positive donor, due to the risk of overwhelming infection (70–80% infection rate; 2% mortality in patients with disseminated disease). However, a CMV-positive recipient could receive a CMV-negative kidney. Pneumocystis typically occurs at 2–4 months.

3.6 C: Fluid intake should be 2 to 3 litres per day

Patients with severe renal impairment usually require fluid restriction in order to avoid peripheral oedema, pulmonary oedema and hypertension. However, in moderate renal impairment, it is usually important to drink 2 to 3 litres per day, in order to excrete the obligatory osmolar load (there is impairment of urinary concentration). There is evidence that moderate protein restriction may help slow progression of chronic renal failure, but severe protein restriction is likely to result in malnutrition and is mainly used to attenuate the symptoms of uraemia in patients unsuitable for dialysis. Patients with chronic renal failure are at increased risk of vascular disease; cholesterol intake needs to be controlled carefully. Patients on a phosphate restriction diet need to limit their intake of dairy products.

3.7 A: Haemodialysis following death cap mushroom ingestion does not affect mortality despite good toxin removal

Peritoneal dialysis is less effective than haemodialysis at toxin removal, and is only indicated where haemodialysis is technically impossible. Highly protein bound toxins such as the tricyclics are not well removed by haemodialysis. Indications for haemodialysis in salicylate poisoning include coma, convulsions and acute renal failure. Use of bicarbonate buffer is mandatory, as acetate will worsen the metabolic acidosis. Death cap mushroom toxicity is not amenable to haemodialysis due to rapid and irreversible end organ damage.

3.8 C: HIV-associated nephropathy typically presents with nephrotic range proteinuria

Renal involvement is rare (3% of autopsies of AIDS patients). The typical histological feature of HIV-associated nephropathy is focal or global capillary collapse. It may respond to zidovudine. The natural history is rapid progression to end stage renal failure. Other features of HIV infection include hyponatraemia, hyperkalaemia and hypocalcaemia.

3.9 D: Penicillamine

Penicillamine works by converting cystine to cysteine-penicillamine, which is 50 times more soluble, hence reducing crystallisation. It should be used in conjunction with a high fluid intake. Alkalisation of the urine is theoretically beneficial, but does not appear to be clinically useful. Cysteamine may be used in the treatment of cystinosis.

3.10 C: Ibuprofen

Thiazides reduce urinary calcium excretion and may be useful in management of idiopathic hypercalciuria.

Corticosteroids are used in the treatment of sarcoidosis, which is associated with calculi formation.

Cholestyramine reduces urinary oxalate excretion in the case of enteric hyperoxaluria.

Pyridoxine may be useful in reducing urinary oxalate excretion in idiopathic hyperoxaluria.

3.11 E: Urine dipstick and microscopy

The patient has rhabdomyolysis following the muscle damage caused by his prolonged convulsion. The low calcium, and markedly elevated potassium, creatinine and phosphate are highly suggestive of this diagnosis. Urine dipstick will test positive for blood (due to the myoglobinuria), but urine microscopy will not demonstrate haematuria. Renal biopsy would confirm the diagnosis more definitively.

3.12 B: Antiglomerular basement membrane disease

The other causes of reduced CH50 in glomerulonephritis are shunt nephritis, type I mesangiocapillary glomerulonephritis, and infective endocarditis.

3.13   A: Adenoma sebaceum in a patient with microscopic haematuria

Accelerated or malignant hypertension, indicated fundoscopically by Grade III or IV changes, may be an aetiological factor in renal failure, but hypertension is of course also an important consequence of renal failure. Adenoma sebaceum (facial angiofibromata) is a typical finding in tuberous sclerosis, a condition characterised by bilateral renal angiomyolipomata and cysts. Deep vein thrombosis is a complication of the nephrotic syndrome. Cushing's syndrome is not typically associated with any renal disease.

Up to 90% of patients with partial lipodystrophy develop progressive glomerulonephritis, most usually mesangiocapillary glomerulonephritis type II. A serum creatinine of 150 μmol/l with normal urinary sediment is an unlikely presentation of this condition.

3.14   A: Infection 2 weeks ago with an alpha haemolytic streptococcus

Poststreptococcal glomerulonephritis is associated with group A beta haemolytic streptococcus. The condition typically occurs 10 to 14 days after upper respiratory tract infection, or 3 weeks after a skin infection.

It typically affects children aged 3–8 years, males more than females. 25% of patients have normal renal function at presentation. 10% of cases have no elevation of ASOT. The proteinuria is typically less than 2 g in 24 hours.

3.15   A: Eclampsia can occur without previous hypertension

Korotkoff phase V may not occur in pregnancy, so it is important to use phase IV. Blood pressure falls in the first trimester, reaches a nadir in the mid trimester, and by term is comparable to non-pregnant blood pressure. This physiological fall is due to reduced vascular resistance, both by vasodilatation, and later due to the uteroplacento circulation. Cardiac output increases by about 40%. The accepted threshold for physiological proteinuria is 0.3 g/24 hr. The risk of pre-eclampsia is 15 times greater for the first pregnancy than the second. Eclampsia occurs without any recognised pre-eclampsia in around 20% of cases.

3.16   C: Severe hyperphosphataemia is a contraindication to the administration of 1, 25 hydroxyvitamin D

The desferrioxamine stimulation test is used to diagnose aluminium overload, which may occur in haemodialysis patients, and is an important cause of renal bone disease.

Cheese is high in phosphate, which should be restricted in renal bone disease. (It is also high in fat, and a major cause of mortality in renal patients is vascular disease.) Phosphate binders must be taken with food, as they bind dietary phosphate. It is important that the phosphate is well controlled before calcitriol is prescribed, otherwise there is the risk of extra-skeletal calcification due to an elevated calcium–phosphate product.

Parathyroidectomy may be necessary in cases of severe tertiary hyper-parathyroidism.

3.17　A: Urinary protein excretion of 3 g/l, in conjunction with microscopic haematuria, may be attributable to strenuous exercise

Pathological levels of proteinuria are a reflection of (a) glomerular pathology, (b) elevated plasma protein levels (overflow proteinuria), or (c) tubular damage (e.g. Fanconi's syndrome). Orthostatic proteinuria disappears during recumbency.

Microalbuminuria is defined as proteinuria greater than the upper limit of normal (150 mg/24 hour) but less than 100 mg/l (threshold for dipstix positivity).

In young adults, the main causes of nephrosis are minimal change disease, focal segmental glomerulosclerosis, proliferative glomerulonephritides, and Henoch–Schönlein disease. Membranous glomerulonephritis is more commonly seen in older patients, due to its association with malignancy.

3.18　C: A 60-year-old man who developed Type 1 DM 43 years ago

Type 1 DM

After development of diabetes, there is a lag period of about five years when development of nephropathy is rare. Thereafter, the annual incidence of the complication increases to a peak of 3% per year 15–17 years after development of diabetes. Patients who have had the disease for more than 35 years have a low risk of developing nephropathy.

Type 2 DM

Unlike Type 1, the incidence of nephropathy rises steadily with time. The patient described in D, is likely to have had undetected diabetes for some time: such patients may present with, or rapidly develop, retinopathy and nephropathy. There is considerable racial heterogeneity with regard to incidence of nephropathy. Japanese and Pima Indians have a cumulative incidence of 50% after 20 years of diabetes, compared with 25% for Caucasians.

3.19　A: Hypercalcaemia

The central feature of haemolytic uraemic syndrome is endothelial injury with platelet adhesion. There is an intravascular haemolytic anaemia, with a fall in haptoglobin, elevated reticulocyte count, thrombocytopenia and neutrophilia. There is usually hyponatraemia.

3.20   A: Acute renal failure in childhood

Peritoneal dialysis is often the modality of choice in childhood. It presents fewer technical difficulties than haemodialysis and the peritoneal membrane is functionally more efficient than in adults. Peritoneal dialysis has a very limited role in removal of poisons.

Relative contraindications to peritoneal dialysis include the following.

- Any previous condition or procedure likely to have caused significant peritoneal scarring.

- Any condition where the splinting of the diaphragm by the dialysate is likely to be deleterious.

- Factors making the patient unable to perform the exchanges safely (only relevant for chronic dialysis i.e. CAPD), such as dementia, poor hygiene, severe arthritis.

- Pre-existing malnutrition, as peritoneal dialysis causes continuous protein loss.

3.21   B: The net insensible water loss is approximately 0.2 l/day

A clinically relevant question! It is important to be able to estimate the insensible losses of a patient accurately. In a normothermic patient, they will be approximately 0.5 l/day. However, this will rise significantly if the patient is pyrexial. Massive fluid volumes can be tolerated acutely in the normal patient. The hyponatraemia seen in psychogenic polydipsia is probably related to impairment of free water excretion.

3.22   A: Cardiac/vascular

Anyone who answered B or E must have little faith in the nephrological service in this country! Malignancy is an important complication of transplantation. Infection is the second greatest cause of death, reflecting both the increased susceptibility of these patients to infection, and the instrumentation they require. However, vascular (including cardiac) causes of death account for 40–50% of all deaths in patients on dialysis. This is partly due to some of the conditions which result in ESRF – diabetes, renal artery disease, and to the increased number of elderly patients now receiving dialysis. However, renal failure itself increases the incidence of atherosclerotic disease, due to hypertension, lipid abnormalities, anaemia, and altered vessel wall characteristics.

3.23   E: 1 g/day proteinuria would be expected with haematuria due to a bladder malignancy

A family history of microscopic haematuria may provide a clue to Alport's syndrome or benign familial haematuria. Only major haematuria (> 50 ml /24 hours) allows enough protein loss into the urine to give a positive result on stix testing. Presence of significant proteinuria should point the clinician firmly towards a renal origin.

3.24   C: Continuous arterio-venous haemofiltration

In order to confirm a diagnosis of hepatorenal syndrome over pre-renal azotaemia, it is often necessary to ensure that there is no reversibility in response to a fluid challenge, and/or to measure the central venous pressure as an estimate of vascular filling. However, once the diagnosis has been made, fluid and sodium restriction are crucial. Whereas orthotopic liver transplantation may be life saving, the kidneys are normal, and do not require transplantation.

Although the renin-angiotensin system is implicated in the pathogenesis of hepatorenal syndrome, trials of the use of ACE inhibitors have resulted in severe hypotension.

Some form of dialysis is often necessary to prevent life-threatening fluid overload, and to permit fluid administration such as bicarbonate or hyperalimentation regimes. However, patients often exhibit too much cardiovascular instability to tolerate haemodialysis, and continuous arterio-venous haemofiltration may be used instead.

3.25   B: Liver ultrasonography of patient

Neonatally, the two conditions are clinically indistinguishable. They are also indistinguishable on renal ultrasonography. Renal ultrasound on the parents will only be conclusive, in the case of a negative examination, if the parents are over the age of 30. There is no indication for IVP or renal biopsy. However, hepatic ultrasound should demonstrate biliary dysgenesis in the case of the recessive condition. Ultimately, genetic studies are most likely to be definitive.

NEPHROLOGY: MULTIPLE CHOICE ANSWERS

3.26   A B C D E

Paracetamol and iron overdose can both cause ATN as will indomethacin. ATN is also seen in ethylene glycol poisoning with the associated histological hallmark of intratubular calcium oxalate crystals. Paraquat causes death in 50% of patients who swallow it and acute renal failure and pulmonary fibrosis are major features of poisoning.

3.27   B D

Urinary sodium excretion may be a useful parameter to distinguish pre-renal uraemia from established ATN. However the main abnormalities that indicate chronic renal disease are small renal size, evidence of long-standing hypertension, established bone disease and normocytic anaemia.

3.28   B

The hepatorenal syndrome results from reduced cortical perfusion secondary to the accumulation of vasoactive substances thought to be either endotoxin or an interleukin, which are normally cleared in the liver. Oliguria and a daily urine sodium excretion of under 10 mmol are the rule. The syndrome only resolves if there is a dramatic improvement in hepatic function and so liver transplantation is the treatment of choice. Interestingly, the kidneys of a patient with hepatorenal syndrome will function if transplanted into a recipient with a normal liver. Although the blood volume is frequently low, plasma expanders rarely improve renal function.

3.29   B

Acute allergic interstitial nephritis is not characteristically associated with hypocomplementaemia; a low serum complement and eosinophilia would suggest atheroembolic disease. Non-oliguric patients usually have less severe renal failure and have a better prognosis. Although dopamine at a dose of 2–5 μg/kg/min may increase renal blood flow this is not necessarily accompanied by a diuresis. Intermittent or partial obstruction both cause nephrogenic diabetes insipidus and may also cause salt wasting.

3.30   A C

Phosphate homoeostasis is influenced by dietary phosphate intake and its re-absorption can be increased when phosphate intake is diminished; the action of PTH leads to phosphaturia. Alkalosis results in kaliuresis, and acetazolamide inhibits both hydrogen ion excretion and bicarbonate re-absorption, leading to acidosis and increased potassium secretion by the distal tubule.

3.31   B C E

Acquired nephrogenic diabetes insipidus is commonly associated with diseases that primarily affect the renal medulla. These include hypokalaemic interstitial nephritis and the recovery phase of ATN. One of the first symptoms of chronic renal failure may be nocturia, which is again due to collecting tubule insensitivity to ADH and the osmotic diuretic effect of raised blood urea.

3.32   A B

The pressure favouring filtration at the glomerulus = hydrostatic pressure – (oncotic pressure + Bowman's capsule pressure) = 45 – (25 + 10) = 10 mm Hg. The basement membrane consists of negatively charged glycoproteins (including sialic acid) and collagen. The filtration fraction = glomerular filtration rate (GFR) divided by renal plasma flow = 125/600 or 20% in normal man. Daily filtration is approximately 180 litres. Efferent arteriolar constriction increases the GFR and may be involved in the phenomenon of 'autoregulation' if renal perfusion pressure falls.

3.33   A D

Glomerular filtration rate increases considerably towards the end of the second trimester and during the third trimester of pregnancy and creatinine usually falls to the lower end of the normal range; this is also manifest by a very low blood urea. The serum concentrations of many nutrients are diminished including the minerals such as magnesium. Rising levels of uric acid in serum are significant and may indicate the onset of pre-eclampsia.

3.34   A C E

The definition of clearance is correct. The clearance of a substance freely filtered but not secreted or reabsorbed by the kidney (e.g. *inulin*) is an accurate estimate of GFR. Renal plasma flow is measured from the clearance of a compound which is filtered and secreted by the kidney (e.g. PAH).

The formula for inulin clearance = $\dfrac{Uin \times V}{Pin}$

where Uin and Pin are the concentrations of inulin in urine and plasma and V is the rate of urine flow/min. Clearance thus calculated is 125 ml/min and is a measurement of the normal GFR. Urea is reabsorbed by the kidney even in the hydrated state (approx. 40%) and the clearance is much lower than the GFR. Probenecid decreases tubular penicillin secretion and hence its renal clearance.

3.35   A B D E

Despite the mechanism of 'autoregulation' which maintains renal blood flow and the GFR within narrow limits, small increases in the renal arterial pressure are paralleled by decreases in proximal sodium re-absorption and sodium excretion is increased. An increase in venous volume stimulates baroreceptors in the atria and in renal capillaries leading to increased sodium excretion by decreased proximal re-absorption and decreased sympathetic tone. Decreased plasma oncotic pressure reduces proximal sodium re-absorption.

3.36   A D E

The reduction in arterial pCO_2 will lower the plasma HCO_3 and increase pH (respiratory alkalosis). The increased pH will reduce the rate of H^+ secretion, less bicarbonate will be reabsorbed and a further fall in plasma HCO_3 will occur. This will correct the pH. The overall response is compensatory as arterial pCO_2 remains low and plasma HCO_3 is much reduced. The main site of bicarbonate re-absorption is proximal.

3.37   B C D E

Renin is a proteolytic enzyme found in the granular cells of the juxta-glomerular apparatus and produced in response to sodium depletion (detected by the cells of the macula densa) or to volume depletion (detected by the atrial and renal capillary baroreceptors). Reduced atrial stretch results in increased renal sympathetic tone and renin release. Renin acts on angiotensinogen (renin substrate) to produce angiotensin I which is converted to angiotensin II, a potent vasoconstrictor which also stimulates thirst. Redistribution of renal blood flow away from the outer cortex stimulates renin release, which may be of relevance to sodium retention in some disease states.

3.38   A B D

The CAPD dialysate contains glucose, the concentration of which varies according to the tonicity of the solution, and its absorption exacerbates obesity – catheter placement may be impossible in the obese patient. Previous abdominal surgery only contraindicates CAPD if adhesions or a potential infection risk such as a stoma or fistula are present. Diaphragmatic splinting with PD fluid can impair ventilation in the patient with chronic pulmonary disease, whereas patients with severe deformity may not possess the dexterity necessary to perform CAPD.

3.39   A C E

Asterixis and hiccoughing are signs of uraemic encephalopathy and so are indications for dialysis. Pericarditis is also life-threatening as cardiac tamponade may occur owing to bleeding from the inflamed pericardium. This may be exacerbated by anticoagulants used during haemodialysis and so reduced heparinization, regional heparinization of the extracorporeal circulation or peritoneal dialysis should be used. Itching is usually a manifestation of secondary hyperparathyroidism and may be worsened acutely during haemodialysis. Peripheral neuropathy seldom resolves even with intensive dialysis, but fortunately is rare nowadays.

3.40   A B D E

Chronic analgesic usage is associated with renal failure, as is retro-peritoneal fibrosis due to methysergide treatment of migraine. Childhood haematuria may be indicative of a progressive glomerulonephritis or of familial renal disease e.g. Alport's syndrome. Chronic exposure to silica (foundry workers) can lead to heavy-metal type interstitial nephritis or glomerulosclerosis.

3.41   A C E

In chronic renal failure there is insulin resistance but urinary calcium excretion is very low. The loss of urinary concentrating ability is an early feature and polyuria may ensue. Metabolic acidosis is a major contributor to the growth retardation of childhood renal failure.

3.42   None correct

The screening test for renal obstruction is ultrasound; if the collecting system is dilated, pressure studies may be needed to confirm the diagnosis. Dehydration may precipitate acute or chronic renal failure owing to contrast nephropathy especially in the elderly, arteriopaths, diabetics and patients with myeloma. The ureters are deviated medially in retroperitoneal fibrosis. Chronically diseased kidneys usually shrink but they characteristically remain large in diabetes, amyloidosis and polycystic kidney disease. Causes of coarse kidney scarring include reflux nephropathy, obstructive uropathy, papillary necrosis and renovascular disease.

3.43   C E

Membranous glomerulonephritis usually presents with moderate to nephrotic range non-selective proteinuria, and granular IgG deposits are seen within the basement membrane of glomeruli. Approximately one third of patients develop end-stage renal failure but the course is usually over several years after diagnosis; adverse prognostic signs at presentation are hypertension and early renal impairment. There is an association with bronchial and gastrointestinal tract malignancy.

3.44   A C E

IgA nephropathy appears more common than other forms of glomerulonephritis, at least in Europe, North America and Australia. Only about 15–25% progress to end-stage renal failure; poor prognostic factors include uraemia at presentation, heavy proteinuria and frequent episodes of macroscopic haematuria. Acute exacerbations usually coincide with infections and are characterised histologically by glomerular crescents, and clinically by loin pain (owing to swelling of the kidney), macroscopic haematuria and heavy proteinuria. The loin pain–haematuria syndrome is a different disease, the aetiology of which is uncertain.

3.45   A B C

Renal vein thrombosis is recognised in the nephrotic syndrome especially when this is due to membranous glomerulonephritis; it may complicate volume depletion in infants. Renal carcinoma can invade the renal veins, predisposing to thrombosis that can propagate into the inferior vena cava.

3.46   A B C

Von Hippel-Lindau syndrome is autosomal dominant and manifests as spinal and cerebellar haemangiomata, renal carcinomas and retinal angiomas. Vesico-ureteric reflux has a familial predisposition but cystinosis is a recessively inherited condition in which chronic renal failure, short stature, eye and cardiac disease are cardinal features. Noonan's syndrome involves a hereditary form of hypertrophic cardiomyopathy with other, non-renal, syndromal associations.

3.47   A B

Vesico-ureteric reflux often only presents as chronic renal failure in adult life; even at this stage ureteric reimplantation may be of benefit for symptomatic reflux. Evidence of urinary tract infection is only present in about 40% of cases.

3.48   A B C D E

Renal tuberculosis may present clinically or radiologically with calculous disease. Since healing is by fibrosis, lesions within the ureter may form strictures especially during the first six weeks of treatment. Active tuberculosis anywhere contraindicates renal transplantation. Transplant recipients with quiescent disease require continuous prophylaxis; isoniazid is preferred to rifampicin since the latter increases metabolism of cyclosporin A. Tuberculous cystitis may cause disabling frequency or dysuria necessitating urinary diversion or a bladder augmentation operation. There is no radiological sign of pulmonary tuberculosis in about 60% of cases.

3.49   A C D

Classical distal renal tubular acidosis (type I) is due to a failure of hydrogen ion excretion into the urine and renal function is well preserved. Nephrocalcinosis or renal tract calculi occur in approximately 70% of cases and the patients have marked hypokalaemia. Typically the urinary pH is > 5.5 and often > 6.0 during acute acidosis. Acquired type I renal tubular acidosis is common with many renal medullary pathologies.

3.50   A B E

Tetracyclines (except doycycline) can exacerbate uraemia by increasing urea generation, whereas non-steroidal anti-inflammatory agents will reduce the glomerular filtration rate in patients with compromised renal perfusion (e.g. cardiac failure, elderly patients during intercurrent illness). The sulphonamide component of mesalazine can provoke interstitial nephritis.

REVISION CHECKLISTS

ENDOCRINOLOGY: REVISION CHECKLIST

Diabetes and glycaemic control
- [ ] Diabetes
- [ ] Hypoglycaemia
- [ ] Glycosylated haemoglobin
- [ ] Hepatic gluconeogenesis
- [ ] Insulinoma

Adrenal disease
- [ ] Cushing's syndrome
- [ ] Addison's disease
- [ ] Congenital adrenal hyperplasia
- [ ] ACTH action

Thyroid disease
- [ ] Thyroxine action/metabolism TFTs
- [ ] Thyroid cancer/nodule
- [ ] Graves' disease/exophthalmos
- [ ] Hypothyroidism

Parathyroid disease
- [ ] PTH/hyperparathyroidism
- [ ] Calcitonin

Pituitary disease
- [ ] Acromegaly
- [ ] Chromophobe adenoma
- [ ] Hyperprolactinaemia
- [ ] Hypopituitarism
- [ ] Pituitary hormones

Miscellaneous

- ☐ Polycystic ovary syndrome/infertility
- ☐ SIADH
- ☐ Short stature
- ☐ Weight gain/Prader-Willi syndrome
- ☐ Endocrine changes in anorexia
- ☐ Hirsutism
- ☐ Hormone physiology (including pregnancy)
- ☐ Sweating

GASTROENTEROLOGY: REVISION CHECKLIST

Liver disease
- ☐ Chronic liver disease
- ☐ Jaundice
- ☐ Primary biliary cirrhosis
- ☐ Gilbert's syndrome
- ☐ Hepatic mass/sub-phrenic abscess
- ☐ Alcohol & liver
- ☐ Portal vein thrombosis

Small bowel disease/Malabsorption
- ☐ Coeliac disease
- ☐ Malabsorption/protein-losing enteropathy
- ☐ Cholera toxin/gastroenteritis
- ☐ Carcinoid syndrome
- ☐ Whipple's disease
      (see also 'Crohn's disease' below)

Large bowel disorders
- ☐ Crohn's disease
- ☐ Ulcerative colitis/colonic carcinoma
- ☐ Irritable bowel syndrome
- ☐ Diarrhoea
- ☐ Inflammatory bowel disease – general
- ☐ Pseudomembranous colitis

Oesophageal disease
- ☐ Gastro-oesophageal reflux/tests
- ☐ Achalasia
- ☐ Dysphagia/oesophageal tumour
- ☐ Oesophageal chest pain

Stomach and pancreas

- ☐ Acute pancreatitis
- ☐ Gastric acid secretion
- ☐ Persistent vomiting
- ☐ Stomach cancer

Miscellaneous

- ☐ GI tract bleeding
- ☐ Abdominal X-ray
- ☐ GI hormones
- ☐ Physiology of absorption
- ☐ Recurrent abdominal pain

NEPHROLOGY: REVISION CHECKLIST

Nephrotic syndrome/related glomerulonephritis
- [ ] Nephrotic syndrome
- [ ] Membranous glomerulonephritis
- [ ] Minimal Change disease
- [ ] Hypocomplementaemia & glomerulonephritis
- [ ] Renal vein thrombosis
- [ ] Acute glomerulonephritis
- [ ] SLE nephritis

Renal failure
- [ ] Acute renal failure
- [ ] Acute versus chronic
- [ ] Chronic renal failure
- [ ] Haemolytic-uraemic syndrome
- [ ] Rhabdomyolysis
- [ ] Anaemia in renal failure
- [ ] Contrast nephropathy

Urinary abnormalities
- [ ] Macroscopic haematuria
- [ ] Discolouration of the urine
- [ ] Nocturia
- [ ] Polyuria

Basic renal physiology
- [ ] Normal renal physiology/function
- [ ] Water excretion/urinary concentration
- [ ] Serum creatinine

Miscellaneous

☐ Distal renal tubular acidosis

☐ Renal papillary necrosis

☐ Diabetic nephropathy

☐ Analgesic nephropathy

☐ Polycystic kidney disease

☐ Renal calculi

☐ Renal osteodystrophy

☐ Retroperitoneal fibrosis

☐ Steroid therapy in renal disease

INDEX

Numbers refer to question numbers

Endocrinology

Acromegaly	1.30	Haemoglobin, glycation	1.19
Addison's disease	1.10	Hair growth, increased	1.12
hormone replacement		Hypercalcaemia	1.16
medication		Hyperparathyroidism	
Anorexia nervosa	1.34	primary	1.18
Antidiuretic hormone	1.31	Hypoglycaemia	1.7, 1.48
Asthma	1.3	Hypoparathyroidism	1.45
acute		Hypopituitarism	1.29
drugs		Insulin-like growth factor-1	1.27
Atrial natriuretic peptide	1.42	Kallmann's syndrome	1.35
Basal bolus insulin	1.25	Medullary thyroid carcinoma	1.21
Calcitonin gene	1.50	Metformin	1.23
Captopril	1.20	Multiple endocrine neoplasia	1.47
Carbohydrate metabolism	1.14	type 2	1.11
Cholesterol	1.15	Paget's disease	1.46
Congenital adrenal hyperplasia	1.44	Pan hypopituitarism	1.2
Craniopharyngioma	1.26	Phaeochromocytoma	1.49
Cushing's syndrome	1.5, 1.41	Pituitary tumour	1.9
cortisol measurements		Polycystic ovarian syndrome	1.6
Diabetes	1.8	diagnostic tests	
with microalbuminuria		Propylthiouracil	1.1
in pregnancy	1.25	Radiotherapy	1.2
Diabetes insipidus	1.32	external beam	
Diabetes type 1	1.7, 1.13	Renal artery stenosis	1.4
'captopril cough'	1.20	Renin level	1.4
Diabetic treatment	1.24	Sickle cell screen	1.19
Diarrhoea	1.21	Sweating	1.21
DIGAMI study	1.24	Synacthen test	1.2
Galactorrhoea	1.33	Testosterone	1.35
Gastrin levels	1.50	Thyroid-binding globulin	1.39
Glucocorticoid		Thyroidism, autoimmune	1.37
replacement	1.43	Thyroiditis, subacute	1.22
treatment	1.10	Thyrotoxicosis	1.38
Glycaemic control	1.23	in pregnancy	1.1
G-proteins	1.40	Trans-sphenoidal surgery	1.9
Graves' disease	1.36		
Growth hormone	1.28		
therapy	1.17		

Gastroenterology

AIDS	2.32	Pancreatitis	
gastrointestinal infections		acute	2.12
Azathioprine	2.14	chronic	2.36
Biliary cirrhosis	2.27	Paracetamol overdose	2.28
primary	2.11	Pernicious anaemia	2.29
Bilirubin	2.43	*Pneumatosis coli*	2.18
Boerhaave's syndrome	2.25	Pseudomembranous colitis	2.35
Caecal cancer investigations	2.5	Rectal ulcer	2.17
Cancer, colorectal	2.31	syndrome	2.39
Cholecystokinin	2.40	Sclerosing cholangitis	2.1
Clostridium difficile	2.50	Thrombosis	2.20
CMV proctitis	2.19	portal vein	
Coeliac disease	2.3, 2.34	Wilson's disease	2.42
Colorectal cancer	2.31		
Copper	2.42		
C-ret oncogene codes	2.44		
Crohn's disease	2.2		
Diarrhoea	2.22, 2.23		
causes			
Dietary fat	2.47		
Folic acid	2.37		
Fulminant hepatic failure	2.10		
Gastric emptying	2.49		
Gastric ulcer, investigations	2.4		
Gastrin	2.26		
Gastrointestinal tract	2.46		
systemic sclerosis			
Gastro-oesophageal reflux	2.45		
GI obstruction	2.7		
Gilbert's syndrome	2.15		
Helicobacter pylori	2.33		
Heller's myotomy	2.24		
Hepatic encephalopathy	2.38		
Hepatitis A	2.10		
Hepatorenal failure	2.9		
Hydatid disease	2.21		
Irritable bowel syndrome	2.6, 2.41		
Mesalazine compounds	2.48		
NICE guidelines	2.8		
Oesophageal varices	2.13, 2.30		
Oesophagitis	2.8		

Nephrology

Arterial pCO$_2$ 3.36
Cholesterol embolisation   3.1
Clearance   3.34
Continuous ambulatory peritoneal
     dialysis   3.38
Cystic disease in neonates   3.25
Cystinuria   3.9
Diabetic nephropathy   3.18
Dialysis   3.7
     peritoneal   3.20
     urgent   3.39
Genetically transmitted diseases
     involving the kidney   3.46
Glomerulonephritis   3.12
     membranous   3.43
     post-streptococcal   3.14
Glomerulus filtration   3.32
     pregnancy   3.33
Haematuria   3.23
Haemolytic uraemic syndrome   3.19
Hepatorenal syndrome   3.24, 3.28
HIV   3.8
     kidney
Hypocomplementaemia   3.12
Hypotension   3.15
     pregnancy
Ibuprofen   3.10
IgA nephropathy   3.44
Kidney   3.30
     hepatitis C   3.2
Penicillamine   3.9
Peritoneal dialysis
     continuous ambulatory   3.38
     in childhood   3.20
Proteinuria   3.17
Renal biopsy findings   3.3
Renal calculi   3.10
Renal disease
     dietary modification   3.6
     end-stage   3.22
     physical signs   3.12

Renal excretion of water   3.31
Renal failure
     acute   3.29
     chronic (moderate)   3.41
     harmful drugs   3.50
     in overdose   3.26
     measurements to distinguish
         acute and chronic   3.27
Renal obstruction   3.42
     screening test
Renal osteodystrophy   3.16
Renal transplant complications   3.5
Renal tuberculosis   3.48
Renal tubular acidosis (type 1)   3.49
Renal vein thrombosis   3.45
Renin   3.37
Rhabdomyolysis   3.11
Rickets   3.4
     vitamin D resistant
Uraemic patient   3.39
     aetiology   3.40
Urinary sodium excretion   3.35
Vesico-ureteric reflux   3.47
Water balance   3.21

PASTEST BOOKS FOR MRCP PART 1

MRCP 1 New Pocket Series
Further titles in this range:
Book 1:   Cardiology, Haematology, Respiratory   *1901198 758*
Book 2:   Basic Sciences, Neurology, Psychiatry   *1901198 804*
Book 4:   Clinical Pharmacology, Infectious Diseases
                Immunology, Rheumatology   *1901198 901*

MRCP 1 New 'Best of Five' Multiple Choice Revision Book
K Binymin   *1901198 57X*
Our new 'Best of Five' Multiple Choice Revision book features subject-based chapters
ensuring all topics are fully covered. Practise new format 'best of five' questions to give
confidence in your ability to sit the exam.

MRCP 1 Multiple True/False Revision Book
P Kalra   *1901198 952*
This book brings together 600 PasTest multiple true/false questions into one volume.
The book is split into subjects but also contains a practice exam so that you can test
your knowledge. Again, detailed teaching notes are provided.

Essential Revision Notes for MRCP Revised Edition
P Kalra   *1901198 596*
A definitive guide to revision for the MRCP examination. 19 chapters of informative
material necessary to gain a successful exam result.

Explanations to the RCP 1997 and 1998 Past Papers
G Rees   *1901198 286*
360 answers and teaching notes to the Royal College of Physicians book of MCQs
from the MRCP Part 1 1997 and 1998 Examinations.

Explanations to the RCP 1990 Past Papers
H Beynon & C Ross   *1901198 576*
180 answers and teaching notes to the Royal College of Physicians book of MCQs
from the MRCP Part 1 1990 Examinations.

MRCP Part 1 MCQs with Key Topic Summaries 2nd edition
P O'Neill   *1901198 073*
200 MCQs with comprehensive key topic summaries bridging the gap between
standard MCQ books and textbooks.

MRCP Part 1 MCQs in Basic Sciences
P Easterbrook & K Mokbel   *1901198 347*
300 exam-based MCQs focusing on basic sciences, with answers and teaching notes.